TONI MORRISON

TONI MORRISON
THE LAST INTERVIEW
and OTHER CONVERSATIONS

MELVILLE HOUSE
BROOKLYN · LONDON

CONTENTS

INTRODUCTION

NIKKI GIOVANNI

I wish I owned a restaurant then I could run Specials: Today Toni Morrison Stew. An exotic mix of tears and sympathy. Nothing grows except The Bluest Eye and a special shot of Pecola which flies over very quickly because no one can really embrace the fear and hatred. The best thing about The Bluest Eye special is the Marigolds. They didn't flower but the seeds are there. Drop a few in the bowl and see what grows. Or doesn't.

I also really recommend the Sula. The mixture of two girl friends who lose each other. It does not come with dessert but it can have hot bread. When the Nel is ready to be taken out of the oven that's the best time to put the Sula in the re-frigerator. Timing is everything with this dish. It has to bal-ance the desire with the impossible. Sometimes the chef will put a bit of college in to mix with that wonderful hat. The hat is a lot of fun because whoever catches it gets a free Song of Solomon and a fresh glass of milk.

Of course we'd mix Jazz Belovedly with a movie and a talk or two. Let's call it The Morrison Café. Vodka, though my preference is cheap champagne. And only bottled water.

If Toni's home had been open to gourmets there would always be porgies frying. Yeah sure everyone thinks fried food is bad for your heart or something but how did the Black Americans get through slavery and segregation without catfish and chitlins? Porgies were a treat. There was a restau-rant in the Village that sometimes had porgies and knowing Toni loved them I would go to New York and pick her up. It was more than a poet could actually afford but she was, after all, Toni Morrison. I had my town car take me up to her home and take us to the café. I still don't know what we talked about but when dinner was over I would ride back to her house. She always said she could call her own town car but I knew my Grandmother would have a heavenly fit if I let Toni go home alone. So I rode up said Good Night and came back to Manhattan. She must have known poets are poorer than novelists but she also knew we both were southerners and there were rules.

I didn't ever know the home that burned down but what I loved about the home on the Hudson was the Nobel Prize citation in the downstairs bathroom. I am fortunate to call Toni Morrison friend. Mostly neither of us had much to say.

There was always a comfortable silence when I visited her. My mother transitioned 24th June then my sister just after that on 5 August. I tried to do what any good daughter and sister would do and I think I got it done. But it was sad. One afternoon I was sitting at my desk just sort of being dismayed when I decided to call Toni. I probably talked more than ever and she was kind enough to listen. She finally said Nikki, Write. That's all you can do. Write.

I wish I had a restaurant then I could also cook up a special Morrison Stew to help us all go through this. The title of this book is The Last Interview but there will never be a last interview with Toni. Her books live and talk to us. She could have said Read. But she said Write. And she is Right.

TONI MORRISON

THE FIRST INTERVIEW: EDITOR'S PERSONAL COMMITMENT SHAPES A SCRAPBOOK OF BLACK HISTORY

BY LILA FREILICHER
PUBLISHERS WEEKLY
DECEMBER 1973

The idea of publishing a nostalgic scrapbook of black history is such a natural that it seems a wonder it wasn't done years ago. Nevertheless it took Random House's vivacious black editor, Toni Morrison, to think of it: "The Black Book" (February 26, $15; paper $5.95), and it took Bill Cosby to describe it: "Suppose a 300-year-old black man had decided, oh, say when he was about 10, to keep a scrapbook—a record of what it was like for himself and his people in these United States. He would keep newspaper articles that interested him, old family photos, trading cards, advertisements, letters, handbills, dreambooks and posters . . . stories, rumors, dates. And he would end up with a journey of Black America: a book just like this one . . ."

No such 300-year-old gentleman was available to Toni Morrison, but she had something almost as good at her disposal—the black memorabilia collections of four men: Middleton (Spike) A. Harris, Morris Levitt, Roger Furman and Ernest Smith, all credited as authors of "The Black Book." Toni supplemented this material with recipes, quotes, stories and other contributions from her friends and relatives—"just plain folks"—because her idea was "to put together a book that the average black person could relate on a personal level." Toni calls this "real black publishing," as opposed to black publishing programs that produce scholarly black histories for a select audience.

Illustrated on every page, "The Black Book" traces the history and culture of black people from their origins in Africa through slavery and freedom, giving examples of black contributions to music, American history, the arts, and sports, and including chapters on folklore and voodoo. There's the New York Caucasian newspaper; a poster proclaiming the "Public Sale of Negroes"; slave owners' records and photos of beatings and lynchings.

But all is not grim. In fact, says Toni, "If I had to summarize the book's main point, I'd say it is survival—triumph despite everything." We see Bessie Smith winning a roller skating contest; Sophie Tucker belting out her theme song, "Some of These Days," written by a black man; Matt Henson, who accompanied Admiral Perry to the North Pole; Frederick Douglass, reared as a slave, who became Marshal of the District of Columbia; and patents testifying to the invention, by blacks, of modern-day fountain pen, the egg beater, street sweeper, corn harvester, and much more. And the book admits, also, to what the jacket copy calls "the ways we failed": ads for Golden Peacock Bleach Crème, Dr. Palmer's Skin Whitener and records of blacks who owned slaves.

Work on "The Black Book" got started last spring after Toni Morrison had completed work on her new novel, *Soula** (Knopf, January 7), and for the last several months the book virtually became a full-time job for her. Even so she managed by working long hours to simultaneously edit books by six other authors. Says Toni, "The designer, Jack Ribik, and production manager, Harold Ragland, and I practically

*   The book was published as *Sula*.

moved in with one another putting the book together page by page. It fell into shape as though it had a life of its own. For example, the poster I found for a New York play about miscegenation, 'The Real Widow Brown,' took on greater meaning juxtaposed with the Virginia black laws. Other photos and posters went well with black poetry and gospel songs, quotes, newspaper clippings, and stories which I had selected and divided into chapter groupings. In this way the material began to speak for itself, with no editorial rhetoric."

Working on "The Black Book" was "a wild and wonderful experience," says Toni. "Everyone I knew was sending me in material. I even called my mother! I got a recipe for tun mush, a 19th century cornmeal concoction, from a cook I know; my aunt wrote up a story on how her sharecropping family escaped North in 1919 with only $30 cash; a friend of mine gave me her uncle's 'dream book' (Did you know that if you dream about bed bugs it means your friends are unfaithful and the number to play is 522?); Author Ishmael Reed sent me his collection of voodoo recipes for keeping a girlfriend faithful, finding lonely people lovers, and triumphing in a lawsuit."

It's obvious that "The Black Book" is a project very close to Toni Morrison's heart. She says, "You have to be black to understand black people's anger, frustration, and enduring hope, so I doubt that any white person could have edited this book. Of course I know it has a certain personal bias in that it contains the material I judged to be most relevant to black history. The result is the kind of book I will be proud to give to my children, I have the confidence that other black people (and white people) will feel the same way."

INTERVIEW WITH TONI MORRISON

INTERVIEW WITH DONALD M. SUGGS JR.
RIVER STYX
1986

DONALD M. SUGGS JR: Your first novel, *The Bluest Eye*, deals with the destruction of a young black girl at the hands of a black community that had adopted white standards of beauty. How did you develop your own literary values in the academic and publishing worlds, both dominated by white standards of excellence?

TONI MORRISON: I think that when I was writing *The Bluest Eye* that idea was uppermost in my mind even in attempting it. It was my desire to read such a book, one that had its own aesthetic integrity. I didn't phrase it in that way. What I thought was that I would like to write a book that didn't try to explain everything to white people or take as its point of departure that I was addressing white people, that the audience for it would be somebody like me. And when that happened certain things just fell away: certain kinds of editorializing, certain kinds of definitions, and to think about the subject matter—those girls—their interior life, my interior life, to do, I suppose, what black musicians have done which is to make judgements myself about what was valuable, what was not valuable, and what was worth saving. That was the impetus for writing it, because I had read a lot of very powerful black literature by men, but I had the feeling they were talking about somebody else. It was not for my enlightenment. It was for clarification . . . It was extremely important for them to do this, for Richard Wright to say, "let me show you America."

SUGGS: Could you elaborate on how the process you've described extends to teaching black students?

MORRISON: That's very difficult because I've done it with mixed classes, but never to an all-black class. It might be interesting to see how that works. But in mixed classes you have an obligation to everyone in the class. So the important thing is not to start with white value systems and then see how blacks reflect off them. The problem has been to start with a black value system and how the texts connection with it or reject it. That was the pedagogical problem, for me to draw up what I think are the characteristics of all black art, the given reality of the black world, which even some black people don't articulate, and the perceived reality. Identify them and then we can go to the books.

SUGGS: Teaching white students must present special problems. How do you approach realities of the black experience which might be commonly accepted in an all-black class?

MORRISON: You start by saying, in the beginning there was dispossession and violence. Then you look at what happened, what positive things came out of that, what black people were able to do with the forms of reclamation and dignity, the forms of that resistance and so on. I take a lot for granted, I used to, rather, and I thought that everybody knew what I meant. But they don't, so I try and say what does it mean to have no self? When the "other" denies it, which is what slavery is, and what do you have to do to reclaim the self or status, and what it means to have no art that you can claim. I just bring in all these quotes from everybody in the world, from then to now, in which it's clear in the criticism that what they're saying is that black Americans don't have anything.

SUGGS: What about black schools? Teaching in that setting, is the task any easier?

MORRISON: It should be. I don't know that it is. Because as a student and a teacher there, those years were pre-Civil Rights years, I left in 1964, were years when the measure of excellence was to outstrip the white schools at one thing or another. Presumably, after Civil Rights curriculum changes were made that were significant and the emphasis was on interior study. I don't know how that turned out. I hear interesting things. I think, for example, that Howard is supposed to be one of the best schools for child development. I don't know what happened to liberal arts. In addition, it was an unfair situation that they were placed in because the hoped-for consequences of Civil Rights were that students could go anywhere. They didn't have to go to Howard for the so-called best education. They could go to other schools, and so could the faculty. They lost the crème de la crème, or whatever the mythological pull was in the '60s when the established, superior white schools started recruiting black kids who didn't have to go to Howard or Fisk or those schools. There were always some who didn't, but I mean in large numbers. So they were in a very difficult position because Howard was always at the forefront of the integrationist fight. And then when that happened you got white kids coming to Howard. You know, the medical school down there is almost two-thirds white.

SUGGS: In your novel, *Sula*, you explore a friendship between two black women, set entirely in the black community. If a woman like Sula were alive today and writing books, how might she reconcile her emphatically black female sensibility with a more mainstream feminist view of relationships and gender?

MORRISON: It would be a little problematic for her. Clearing the field for some intelligent discussion of gender, and say, feminist problems are important. It's not a cul-de-sac. It's not an aim in itself. And a world deprived of male sensibilities is an incomplete world. So it's very delicate. It's not a line. It's where two things come together and touch. Each one, hopefully, is enhanced by its relationship to the other. What I'm trying to say is that white feminist views are in some areas so problematic for me, since I'm going to assume that I can do what Sula would do. If she was unorthodox enough, she probably would be interested in unorthodox, or at least non-mainstream solutions. But then she might not.

The divisiveness is unfortunate, that we have words like "either/or" in the vocabulary that are taken too seriously. I think that forced to make a choice between my sons and feminists . . . If I do, it will not be the latter. But I don't know why I have to make that choice, and I refuse to. It's like abortion and right to life, as though there were an inevitable conflict there. There isn't. But it's being drawn up as a battleground when it doesn't exist. Nobody is saying you have to do this.

The idea of conflicting modes of life existing in the same place has always been a troublesome thing in this country. People are always drawing up sides and battle grounds. And the other side should be killed. It can't contain two points of view in a harmonious society. That is just the way we are educated toward conflict and destruction. Because if you're proven right and the other person is wrong, then wrong means death. You can't exist. As a woman with X and Y chromosomes, it seems to me that what women ought to be able to do it make reconciliations among these various types. The idea of ideological slaughter of the other is chewing up everybody's intelligence. People are making the most unbelievable statements about the other based on that kind of insistence that the person who disagrees with you fundamentally can't exist. These are political statements as well as biological and everything else. The hierarchy being established is what's problematic. So there are those who want to accommodate themselves into a man's world, those who want to take over the freedom and access of a man's world, and those who want to exclude men entirely from the world that they live in. They run the gamut, it seems to me, all based on some hostility. Not that they're not legitimate complaints. The enemy is not men. The enemy is the concept of patriarchy, the concept of patriarchy as the way to run the world or do things is the enemy, patriarchy in medicine, patriarchy in schools, or in literature.

SUGGS: You've said that you feel that questions about the role of black women are best examined in the context of the black experience. How do you respond to criticism of what is sometimes seen as an unfair portrayal of black men in the world of black women writers?

MORRISON: Women writers, some of them, are very sensitive to the special considerations of black males in white, patriarchal society. Because of the intimacy, they understand the nature of racism and they do not lump black men in the category of simply alien men. Others of them seem to, but I don't find it as strident among black women as I do among white women. When you see a very militant white feminist, it's very exclusive. They tend not to permit male sensibilities in their world. I don't find that as strong among black women. Although people tell me, and I guess that perhaps they're right, because I'm not familiar with all of it, that black men complain about the kind of men in literature that black women write. Nobody's tender and nobody's reasonable. But I think that they're mistaken. I think that Paule Marshall doesn't write about men that way. I certainly don't. Some of them are terrible and some of them are nice. Tony Cade Bambara doesn't write about men that way. Gloria Naylor doesn't write about men that way. So I think that they're misinformed, because there are those who—whenever they see that men are not wonderful—get alarmed. Their sensitivity is real. They should be sensitive, because no one should take the easy route when describing male characters. There are some books in which black men are just foils for the women's growth. And you don't believe them for a minute. It may be useful for your story, but I don't believe it. So men have a right to be alert and sensitive to that problem, just as we have a right to be sensitive to the opposite problem, of how black women are treated in the books of black men.

SUGGS: An interviewer once asked you about the effect of the number of one-parent families on the black community. Could you expand on your answer that black women could use the absence of a man as a resource for independence?

MORRISON: I believe that suggesting that a one-parent family is crippled in some way is somebody else's notion. I do know that no one parent can raise a child completely. But it is also true that two parents can't do it either. You need everybody. You need the whole community to raise a child. And one parent can get that community. You have to work at it. You have to decide. I mean community, not meaning neighborhood the way it was meant when I was a little girl. There was a street and a block. That doesn't exist now for most of us, particularly if you're a single working parent. You have to collect around you the people who can serve that function for you, and provide multiple kinds of resources for your children. I have women friends who raise their children alone and are working, whose children relate to her friends like family members. They call on one another in times of crisis and duress. They really use each other as a kind of life-support system, so that you don't have this kind of single, one-on-one relationship that is too tense for the child and too tense for the parent. Nobody can deliver that much. The parent can't and the child can't, so you do need these other people. You need a tribe. I don't care what you call it, extended family, large family. That's what one needs.

SUGGS: Alice Walker has criticized books which she felt had "white folks on the brain." What effect might it have on the works of black women writers who have been commercially successful largely due to whites at the bookstore cash register?

MORRISON: There is an advantage to having a wide relation-ship, both black and white, which is that it makes it possible for lots of other writers to get published. Once there's a mar-ket—and you have to remember that the whole system is con-trolled by whites—once that readership exists, then it's likely that other black writing will be purchased by companies and distributed and sold. That is important. As far as it affects the writings, it can't. I suppose one could let it. Writing for the gallery is something that a writer must resist no matter who he is. You know the writers that are writing for their audience because they write the same book over and over again with the sort of cute things their readership likes. Serious writers write things that compel them, new challenges, new situa-tions, and a new landscape that they have not been in before. But I had always made sure from the beginning that the ad-dress of the novel would be interior, that I would writer for a reader who wanted what I wanted, and I could put myself up as a person whose demands were at least different and then would be higher and higher. But paradoxically, what happens is that the more specific one is, the more specificity there is in the writing, the more accessible it is. Tolstoy was not writ-ing for little colored girls in Ohio. He was writing Russian, specifically upper-class things about certain situations and so on. And so was everybody who was of any interest. That subtle racist argument about how universal art works better than any other is fraudulent entirely. Anybody who sets out and writes a universal novel has written nothing. The more concentrated it is in terms of its culture the more revealing you find it, because you make those connections. You see, there are more connections among us than differences, and that is the point. You don't wipe out a culture. You don't wipe out the ethnic quality. You certainly don't address yourself to a parallel or dominant culture. Some black writers did. Much of what was written during the Harlem Renaissance was written with white readers in view, very sort of "let me show you how exotic I am." You can always hear that voice. That may be what she meant. There are contemporary writers who do it still. I don't think that readership has anything to do with it. I suppose there may be black writers who have a large white readership who write for that readership, but I can't imagine it. That only happens on television. You have these little comic book things. You try and straddle some line where it's this, but really it's that. It's blackface really. It may be in different dress, but that's what it is, black people playing black people. It's interesting though that there are a lot of women who write books with an audience of men in mind. I can feel when they're getting over on some man. He looms too large. What is this? The wilder they get in their approbation, the more important he must have been. That's a mighty big gun, isn't it, for just that little character over there? A big Gatling gun they used to call it, just to blow this little man away. So really he must have been important. The gun's just too big.

TONI MORRISON ON CAPTURING A MOTHER'S 'COMPULSION' TO NURTURE IN *BELOVED*

INTERVIEW WITH CHARLAYNE HUNTER-GAULT
PBS NEWSHOUR
1987

As one of America's most formidable women of letters, Toni Morrison always gets a lot of attention when a novel of hers is published. Her latest, *Beloved,* came out in September, and is already in its third printing. It's fast moving to the top of the bestseller list, following the pattern of Morrison's four other novels published over the last sixteen years: *The Bluest Eye, Sula, Song of Solomon*, and *Tar Baby.* When *Tar Baby* was published in 1981, Morrison's stature in the world of fiction earned her a *Newsweek* cover story. *Beloved* is the second Morrison novel to become a Book of the Month Club main selection.

Beloved is the story of the runaway slave, Sethe, who tries to kill her children rather than see them return to slavery. She succeeds in killing only one: a daughter named Beloved. The story unfolds around the return of *Beloved*'s angry ghost. She moves into the house with her mother and sister, Denver. Here, Morrison reads from a passage that illuminates Denver's view of the murder, and Sethe's need to make Beloved's ghost understand it.

CHARLAYNE HUNTER-GAULT: Toni Morrison, what inspired this theme?

TONI MORRISON: I'd read an article, in a nineteenth-century newspaper, about a woman whose name was Margaret Garner, who had indeed killed or tried to kill her children. She was a fugitive slave, and rather than have them go back, she decided to take them all into a permanent place of oblivion. And it was an article that stayed with me for a long, long time, and seemed to have in it an extraordinary idea that was worthy of a novel, which was this compulsion to nurture, this ferocity that a woman has to be responsible for her children. And at the same time, the kind of tensions that exist in trying to be a separate, complete individual.

HUNTER-GAULT: You've said that she has no, she *had* no right to do it, but I would've done the same thing, I mean—

MORRISON: It was the right thing to do . . . [*Laughing*] but she had no right to do it. I think I felt the claims—you see, those women were not . . . parents. They could have—well, people insisted that they have children, but they could not be mothers because they had nothing to say about the future of those children, where they went, they could make no decisions, they fricking couldn't even name them. So that they were denied humanity in a number of ways, but they were denied *that* role, which is . . . uhm . . . early . . . uhm . . . I mean, it has nothing to do with history. It's what women do. And so, she claimed something that she had no right to claim, which the property—her children—and claimed it so finally that she decided that she could not only dictate their lives but end them. And when one knows what the life—what their future would be—her decision is not that difficult to understand.

HUNTER-GAULT: You've talked about previous accounts of slavery being simplistic, and not probing the interior being of the characters. Is this—how difficult was it for you to probe the interior being of characters, albeit black, still from a long, long time ago?

MORRISON: Exactly. Well, my disappointment in some of the accounts, uh, was based on the fact that this is so large, you see. And then the big problem is that slavery is so you intricate, so immense, and so *long*, and so unprecedented, that you can let slavery be the story, the plot. And you know what that story is. And it is predictable. And then you do the worst thing, which is you de—you—the center of it becomes the institution and not the people. So, if you focus on the characters and their interior life, it's like putting the authority back into the hands of the slaves, rather than the slave owner.

HUNTER-GAULT: What is the rationale for the ghost?

MORRISON: First of all, I really wanted her past, her memories, her haunting memories, not to be abstract. I wanted her to actually sit down at the table with the things she's been trying to avoid and explain away, which is this past, this terrible thing that happened, to confront it. As a way of saying that's what the past is. It's a living thing. It's this relationship between ourselves and our personal history, and our racial history, and our national history, that sometimes gets made, you know, sort of distant. But if you make it into a person then it's an inescapable confrontation. The other was that it was part of the milieu of black people to think in terms of a very intimate relationship between the living and the dead. They didn't have that, you know, sort of modern dismissal— they didn't dismiss those things.

HUNTER-GAULT: This book, *Beloved*, has received almost, uh, no, uh, *critical*, uhm, reviews. I mean, just total acclaim. But one of the things that critics have said both about this book in the character of Sethe and other works of yours is that you draw characters that are larger than life. Does that disturb you, or is that even a criticism as far as your concerned?

MORRISON: It used to disturb me. But I realized that what they are saying is that life is small. My characters are not bigger than life. They are, in fact, *as* big *as* life. And life is really very big. We tend to cut it down these days, smaller and smaller and smaller, to make it fit—I don't know what—a headline or a room.

HUNTER-GAULT: Do you think that modern readers have a diminished view of life?

MORRISON: The readers don't, but the writers are making it smaller and smaller.

HUNTER-GAULT: Why? Television?

MORRISON: Maybe so. We've been cut down to screen size, and to short articles. Dwelling in the life of a complicated person, over a complicated period, in *fiction*, is not in vogue. It's shorter, it's smaller, it's a narrower geography. One can do it in history and biography, but not in contemporary life.

HUNTER-GAULT: You said many years ago—well, not *many* years ago, back in the seventies—that—you were an editor at that time at Random House—and you were saying that you wanted to participate in developing a canon of black work beyond black self-flagellation, the kind of entertainment that you felt was being encouraged among black writers by white editors or the white society. Did you succeed in particular, and has the publishing world succeeded in general, in having a better balance of work?

MORRISON: A little. There's still resistance, because the fix on who that reader is hasn't changed a great deal, uh, the reader is somebody between forty and sixty who's white and lives, you know, in a suburb near a big city—the sort of classic profiles of who buys books. But something happened in the meantime, and a huge readership emerged—black and white and female—which made a difference in what was published. When I mentioned the self-flagellation I was particularly aware of some titles in particular, but more importantly the eagerness with which publishers and, uh, people in the book industry were interested in books by black people that said, 'Let me . . . tell me how angry how are. Let me see your anger. Tell us how terrible it has been for you.' And so there was a sly encouragement to sort of expose the horrors of being victim, which some people played into. But it was like feeding the vampire with one's own blood. Instead of describing, you know, a complicated, extraordinary, uh, *survival* life. Which doesn't mean you wipe the slate clean and all the black people are heroic—and there was a mood of that. But you have some—what I regard as some of the most complicated and interesting and mysterious people in the world. A whole group of them. And they need to be revealed for what *that* life is. Not simply to reveal, and educate, or even play into the hands of the yearning—what *used* to be a yearning—for the guilt, expressions of guilt by white people. And that's what I meant by that, sort of, large book. And I wanted that to change. And many black women writers have succeeded along those lines because there was this active growing readership out there who was just desperately hungry to see themselves set the stage for change.

HUNTER-GAULT: What happens as a Toni Morrison who has been responsible for introducing so many new voices into American fiction, letters . . . as you move farther and farther away from your editing responsibility because of the success of your own publishing, uhm, who fills that void? And what does that—how does that make you feel? I mean, [*Laughing*] in a way you are abandoning your children!

MORRISON: [*Laughs*] It's true, I am abandoning them as an editor. But I am convinced that the more I am well known—the better known I am—the easier it is for other writers to come along. If I till that soil myself, in publicity, travelling around Europe, selling books, lecturing, what have you, then all of the younger people who won't have to break down those same doors, they'll be open. They will write infinitely better than I do. They will write of all sorts of things that no one writer can ever touch. They will be stronger, and they will be *delicious* to read. But part of that availability and accessibility is because six or seven black women writers, among whom I am one, have already been there and tilled the soil.

TONI MORRISON ON LOVE AND WRITING, AND DEALING WITH RACE IN LITERATURE

INTERVIEW WITH BILL MOYERS
PBS TV
MARCH 11, 1990

BILL MOYERS: [voice-over] Toni Morrison seems always to be in two worlds. There is the visible world, bustling around her, and there is the world of her novels, whose characters tell us about an interior reality hidden from the eyes of strangers.

In her five books, she has transported millions of readers into the experience of being black in America. *The Bluest Eye*, *Sula*, *Song of Solomon*, *Tar Baby*. In *Beloved*, perhaps the most painful and beautiful of her creations, Toni Morrison reached back into the 19th-century years of slavery.

Her writing has won numerous awards, including the National Book Critics Circle Award for *Song of Solomon* in 1978, and the Pulitzer Prize for *Beloved* in 1988. Fifteen universities have awarded her honorary degrees.

Like many fiction writers, Morrison has earned a living by other means. She was an editor for Random House, and taught at Howard University, Yale, and the State University of New York at Albany. She is now teaching in the humanities at Princeton University.

She is also a trustee at the New York Public Library, where we talked about how the invented world of fiction connects to life as it is.

[interviewing] There is such a gulf between the "inner city" today and the rest of the country, in both imagination and reality and politics and literature; frankly, very little communication takes place. If you were writing for the rest of the country about the inner city today, what metaphor would you use? And I ask that question because you struck a common metaphor in *Song of Solomon*, the metaphor there was flying, everybody's dream of literally being up and away in the air, all of us could identify with that. But what, if you were writing for the rest of the country, would you use as a metaphor for the inner city today?

TONI MORRISON: Love. We have to embrace ourselves. Self-regard. I remember James Baldwin said once, "You've already been bought and paid for, your ancestors already gave it up for you. It's already done. You don't have to do that anymore. Now you can love yourself. It's already possible." So I have this feeling of admiration and respect and love for these black people in the inner city who are intervening, who are going in and saying, "You four girls, you come to my house every Thursday and we're going to eat, we're going to take you out." I mean, these are professional women, we'll say, who go in, have these companions.

I love those men I heard about in Chicago, black professional men who went every lunch hour to the playgrounds in Chicago's South Side to talk to those children. Not to be authoritarian, but just to get to know them, without the bureaucracy, without the agencies, to simply become an agency.

MOYERS: The love you're talking about is the love inspired by moral imagination that takes us beyond blood.

MORRISON: Absolutely. Absolutely that.

MOYERS: But the image one has—and as a reporter, I've been there—that in so many of these neighborhoods, that simply is impossible—

MORRISON: Is lacking.

MOYERS: —because of the wasted nature.

MORRISON: Mm-hmm. It's terrible. It's terrible. It's absolutely terrible. It reminds you of some nightmare that the Marquis de Sade thought up, in some of those places. But the children—I call them children when they're under 18—are hungry for that love. The drugs are just a sleep that you can't even wake up from, because you might remember what you did when you were there. There's no place for them—there should be a rehabilitation center on every corner, along with McDonald's and the banks. This is serious business. The waiting lists are incredible. I mean, it's terrible. It's really terrible.

But, some interesting things have happened along that line. Some woman told me a couple of weeks ago, a close friend of mine, that men, black men, were going into shelters, I think. They were spending time holding crack babies, I mean children who were born—holding them. Holding them. Now, I'm sure it does something for the baby, but think what it does for that man, to actually give up some time and hold a baby.

MOYERS: I remember that John Leonard once said, "Toni Morrison writes about places where even love found its way with an ice pick." Maybe that's the—can we talk about love for a moment?

MORRISON: Sure.

MOYERS: You say love is a metaphor, and when I go back through the novels, love is there in so many different ways and forms that—and particularly when I look at the women in your novels, at the extraordinary things they do for love. There's the grandmother who has her leg amputated so that she can have an insurance policy that will buy a house and take care of her children as they grow up. There's Sethe, who is willing to kill her children before the slave catchers can come and seize them. What kind of love is that?

MORRISON: Some of it's very fierce. Powerful. Distorted, even, because the duress they work under is so overwhelming. But I think they believed, as I do, while it may be true that, you know, people say, "I didn't ask to be born," I think we did, and that's why we're here. We are here, and we have to do something nurturing that we respect before we go. We must. It is more interesting, more complicated, more intellectually demanding and more morally demanding to love somebody, to take care of somebody, to make one other person feel good.

Now the dangers of that are the dangers of setting oneself up as a martyr or as, you know, the one without whom it would not be done.

MOYERS: Paul Deas says to Sethe, "Your love is too thick." Is that what you're talking about here?

MORRISON: Too thick. That's right. It can get to be very excessive.

MOYERS: And how do we know when a love is too thick?

MORRISON: We don't, we really don't. That's a big problem. We don't know when to stop, as Baby Suggs says, "When is it too much and when is it not enough?" That is the problem of the human mind and the soul. But we have to try that. We have to try that. We have to do that. And not doing it is so poor for the self. It's so poor for the mind. It's so uninteresting to live without that, and it has no risk. There's no risk involved. And that just seems to make life not just livable, but a gallant, gallant event.

MOYERS: But I have the sense, in so many of the love stories in your novels—that the world is destined to doom love, or that love is destined to be doomed by the world.

MORRISON: Well, in the stories, the characters are placed by me on a cliff. I mean, I sort of push them as far as I can, to see of what they are made.

MOYERS: I don't think I've ever met a more pathetic creature in contemporary literature than Pecola Breedlove, in *The Bluest Eye*, the little girl who wants the blue eyes. Abused by her—

MORRISON: Everybody.

MOYERS: —parents, rejected by her neighbors, ugly, homely, alone. Finally descending into madness. But I—it's been years since I read that novel, but I remember her.

MORRISON: She surrendered completely to the so-called master narrative.

MOYERS: To?

MORRISON: The master narrative, I mean, the whole notion of what is ugliness, what is worthlessness, what is contempt. She got it from her family, she got it from school, she got it from the movies, she got it everywhere.

MOYERS: The master narrative. What is—that's life?

MORRISON: No, it's white male life. The master narrative is whatever ideological script that is being imposed by the people in authority on everybody else. The master fiction. History. It has a certain point of view. So, when these little girls see that the most prized gift that they can get at Christmastime is this little white doll, that's the master narrative speaking. "This is beautiful, this is lovely, and you're not it." So if you surrender to that, as Pecola did, the little girl, the eye of the story, is sort of a bridge there, and they're sort of resistant, a little feisty about it. They don't trust any adults. She is so needful, so completely needful, has so little, needs so much, she becomes the perfect victim, the total, you know pathetic one. And for her, there is no way back into the community and in society. For her, as an abused child, she can only escape into fantasy, into madness, which is part of what the mind is always creating, we can think that up.

MOYERS: What about Ella, in *Beloved*, who says, "If anybody was to ask me, I'd say don't love nuthin'."

MORRISON: "Don't love nuthin'." I've heard that said a lot, "Don't love nuthin', save it." You see, that was the—one of the devastating things, I think, in the experience of black people in this country, was the effort to prevent that, the full expression of their love. And that sentiment that Ella has is conservative, if you want to hang on to your sanity, hang on to yourself, don't love anything, it'll hurt. And of course, that's true not just of African Americans, it's true of all sorts of people. It's so risky. People don't want to get hurt. They don't want to be left. They don't want to be abandoned, you see. It's as though love is always some present you've given somebody else. And it's really a present you're giving yourself.

MOYERS: On the other hand, there's Pilate, your character who reminds me of my Aunt Mildred, who says in *Song of Solomon*, "I wish I'd knowed more people. I would have loved them all. If I'd a knowed more, I would have loved more." There are people like that, too. Not all of your characters are driven by dark insanity.

MORRISON: No, but that's a totally generous, free woman. Fearless. She's not afraid of anything. She has a few little things. She has a little vaguely supportive skill that she can perform. She doesn't run anybody's life. She's available for almost infinite love, almost infinite. If you need her, she'll deliver. And complete clarity about who she is, complete clarity.

MOYERS: Do you know people like that?

MORRISON: Yes. In my family. Women who presented themselves to me that way. They were just absolutely clear, and absolutely reliable. And they had this sort of intimate relationship with God and death and all sorts of things that strike fear into the modern heart. They had a language for it. They had a—I don't know, a blessedness, maybe. But they seemed not to be fearful. It's to those women, you know, that I really feel an enormous responsibility whenever I answer questions such as the ones you've put to me and about how terrible it all is, how it's all going down the drain. I think about my great-grandmother, and her daughter and her daughter, and all those women who had—I mean, incredible things happened to those people. They never knew from one day to the next about anything. But they believed in their dignity, that they were people of value, that they had to pass that on. And they did it, so that when I confront these sort of, oh, 20th-century problems, look at—

MOYERS: These sort of little 20th-century problems? But you seem to have defined one of them quite interestingly, the conflict of identity between Nell and Sula.

MORRISON: Sula, yes.

MOYER: Nell gives herself to the community, needs the security, the comfort, the conformity of it. And Sula comes along, as you said—

MORRISON: Destructive, yeah.

MOYERS: She's out there, independent, self-uncontained and uncontainable, you said. Now, you call her the new black woman, the New World black woman.

MORRISON: New World, yeah.

MOYERS: Why?

MORRISON: Well, she's experimental, she's sort of an outlaw. I mean, you know, she's not going to take it anymore. I mean, she's at the—she's available to her own imagination. She's available to her own imagination. And other people's stories, other people's definitions, are not hers. The interesting thing about Sula is that she makes you do your own defining for yourself, So I was putting together two sort of strands of womanhood. Certainly black womanhood is a nurturing black neighborhood woman who relies on that, but without the imagination of the New World, and then Sula, who doesn't have the other roots, has no seed around which to grow. I happen to think that they need each other. I mean, that the New World black woman needs a little of the Old World black woman in her, and the other way around. I don't think that they are completely fulfilled without the other. I think an ideal situation is a Sula who has some responsibilities and takes them upon herself, but at the same time has this, you know, flair. I don't like those either/or scenarios where you do this, and you can't do that. I think one of the interesting things that certainly feminine intelligence can bring is a kind of a look at the world as though you can do two things, or three things—the personality is more fluid, more receptive. The boundaries are not quite so defined. And I think that's part of what modernism is.

MOYERS: A creation of a new kind of person who, like Nell, is committed to nurture and caring.

MORRISON: Yeah, that you can rely on.

MOYERS: But like Sula, is defiant of the master narrative. I mean, she won't let it write her script for her. She writes her own rules so that she can defy them.

MORRISON: Exactly.

MOYERS: There's a combination there that we hope emerges.

MORRISON: Yeah. If you see a—you know, if it happens—and I think I have seen women who strike me as being like that—you've had guests on your program who looked like that, women who are very independent, very fierce, artist women, black women, who at the same time, you know, can cook and sew and nurture and manage and so on. And I think that we're probably in a very good position to do that, as black women. I mean, we're managing households and other people's children and two jobs and listening to every-body, and at the same time, creating, singing, holding, bear-ing, transferring the culture, for generations. We've been walking on water for 400 years. So now there's the 20th cen-tury. We don't have to jettison that, like, say, Jadine in *Tar Baby* and go off and totally westernize, Europeanize oneself. Nor do we have to be her aunt, Ondine. There's something in between. There's something in between, and that's what's really attractive and challenging. And since you can feel both worlds sort of pressing on one, it's an ideal space for African American women to inhabit.

MOYERS: Have these women you have created taught you anything?

MORRISON: Oh, yeah . . . All the books are questions for me. I mean, they start out—I write them because I don't know something. I don't—I want to know what does that feel like, that color thing, that—in *The Bluest Eye*, what does that feel like, to really feel that worthlessness? And the same thing is true with *Sula* and *Song of Solomon*, to all of them, was there was something in there I really did not understand? I really didn't know. What is the problem between a pair of lovers who really love one another but have culturally different—I mean, is that what that battle is about, culture, class, in *Tar Baby*, when Son and Jadine can't speak to one another? They're all sort of right, but nobody will give. Nobody will say, "Okay, I'll give you this little bit." What do they learn? How can you manage to love another person under these circumstances, if your culture, your class, your education is that different? You know, where is the ground? And I—all the while I wrote that book I was so eager for them to make it, you know, sort of end up and get married and go to the seashore.

MOYERS: And yet—

MORRISON: They didn't. They all had to learn something else, I think, before that would happen. And with Beloved, oh, I began to think about, really, motherhood and,—you know, it's not the all-encompassing role for women now; it can be a secondary role, or you don't have to choose it. But on the other hand, there was something so valuable about what happens when one becomes a mother. For me, it was the most liberating thing that ever happened to me, having children.

MOYERS: Liberating?

MORRISON: Oh.

MOYERS: Most—the clichés say, well, you're immediately imprisoned by the love that you want to give, but you are a hostage to that love and to those small children and to their lives. You now define yourself like whites and blacks used to do with each other, by children. They are "-" you're limiting yourself. But you're saying liberating.

MORRISON: Liberating. Because of—the demands the children make are not the demands of a normal other. The children's demands on me were things that nobody else ever asked me to do.

MOYERS: Such as?

MORRISON: Be a good manager, have a sense of humor; deliver something that somebody can use. And they were not interested in all the things that other people were interested in, like what I was wearing, or, you know, if I was sensual, or if I was—you know, all of that went by. You've seen those eyes of those children. They don't want to hear it. They want to know, what are you going to do now, today? And somehow, all of the baggage that I had accumulated as a person about what was valuable, so much of that just fell away. And I could not only be me, whatever that was, somebody actually needed me to be that. It's different from being a daughter.

You know, you figure out how to do that. Or it's different from being a sister. Those children could listen to them, look at them, they make demands that you can live up to. Not you can't, because they don't need all that overwhelming love, either. I mean, that's just you being vain about it. If you listen to them, somehow you are able to free yourself from baggage and vanity and all sorts of things and deliver a better self, one that you like. The person that was in me, that I liked best, was the one my children seemed to want. That one. The one, when they walked in the room, do you frown at the children and say, "Pull your socks up," or is their presence, you know—also, you begin to see the world through their eyes, again, which are your eyes. I found that extraordinary. It is true that it is physically confining, you can't go anywhere. You have to be there.

MOYERS: You raised them by yourself, didn't you?

MORRISON: Yes.

MOYERS: Would you have liked to have had the help of a companion?

MORRISON: Yes. It would have been just somebody else to think that, too. Yes, it would have been nice. The more the merrier. I needed a lot of help.

MOYERS: As I listen to you talk about the liberation of motherhood and love, I find all the more incredible Sethe's willingness to kill her son—

MORRISON: Oh, yeah.

MOYERS: —rather than let the slavecatcher kidnap him. Was that a far-out figment of your imagination to make a dramatic point, or did you find in your research into the past there were mothers willing to do that?

MORRISON: That was Margaret Garner's story. There was a slave woman in Cincinnati named Margaret Garner who escaped from Kentucky; arrived in Cincinnati with her mother-in-law. The situation was a little different; I think she came with four others. And right after she got there, the man who owned her found her. And she ran out into the shed and tried to kill all her children, just like that. And she was about to bang one's head against the wall when they stopped her. Now, she became a cause celebre for the Abolitionists, because; you see, they were trying to improve the situation a little bit and get her tried for murder, because that would have been a big coup, if they had gotten her tried for murder. Because it would assume that she had some responsibility over those children. But they were not successful. She was tried for the real crime, which was stolen property, and convicted and returned to that same man.

But what struck me, because I didn't want to know a great deal about her story because there would be no space for me to invent—was that when they interviewed her, she was not a mad dog killer, she was this very calm, you know, in her 20s, woman. And all she said was, "They will not live like that. They will not live like that." And her mother-in-law, who was a preacher, said, "I watched her do it, and I neither encouraged her nor discouraged her." So for them, it was a dilemma. This is a real dilemma. "Shall I permit my children, who are my best thing, to live like I have lived, and I know that's terrible, or to take them out?" So she decided to kill them, and kill herself. And that was noble. That was the identification. She was saying: "I'm a human being. These are my children. This script I am writing."

MOYERS: Could you have put your—did you ever put yourself in her position, and ask—

MORRISON: In the writing of the book, yeah.

MOYERS: —could I have done that to my three sons?

MORRISON: I asked it a lot. As a matter of fact; the reason the character Beloved enters is because I couldn't answer it. I felt just like Baby Suggs. I didn't know whether I would do it or not. You hear stories of that in slavery and Holocaust situations, I mean, where women have got to figure it out fast, I mean really fast. So the only person I felt who had the right to ask her that question was the child she killed.

MOYERS: The child.

MORRISON: And she can ask her: "What did you do that for? Who are you talking about? This is better? What do you know?" Because I just—it was, for me, an impossible decision. Someone gave me the line for it at one time, which I have found useful, is that it was the right thing to do, but she had no right to do it.

MOYERS: And you've never answered it in your own case, "Could I do it?"

MORRISON: I've asked. I don't know.

.   .   .

BILL MOYERS: *[voice-over]* Toni Morrison seems always to be in two worlds. There is the visible world bustling around her, and there is the world of her novels, whose characters tell us about an interior reality hidden from the eyes of strangers. In her five books, she has transported millions of readers into the experience of being black in America: *The Bluest Eye, Sula, Song of Solomon, Tar Baby*. In *Beloved*, perhaps the most painful and beautiful of her creations, Toni Morrison reached back into the 19th-century years of slavery.

Her writing has won numerous awards, including the National Book Critics Circle Award for *Song of Solomon* in 1978, and the Pulitzer Prize for *Beloved* in 1988. Fifteen universities have awarded her honorary degrees. Like many fiction writers, Morrison has earned a living by other means. She was an editor for Random House and taught at Howard University, Yale, and the State University of New York at Albany. She is now teaching in the humanities at Princeton University. She is also a trustee at the New York Public Library, where we talked about her widely noted essay in the *Michigan Quarterly Review* discussing the Afro-American presence in American literature.

[interviewing] You said in your lecture at the University of Michigan that it's a great relief to you that terms like "white" and "race" are now discussable in literature. How so?

TONI MORRISON: Because a language had been developed—and has still some sovereignty—in which we mean *white* and we mean *black*, or we mean *ethnic*, but we say something else. And so there's an enormous amount of confusion. It's difficult even to understand the literature of the country if you can't say *white* and you can't say *black* and you can't say *race*. One of the things I was doing in that speech was using some of the scholarship that other Africanist scholars had already done, in order to say at last, we can look clearly, for example, at Herman Melville. At Edgar Allan Poe. At Willa Cather. At real issues that were affecting founding as well as 20th-century

American writers, because now it's not incoherent, because we can talk about it now. We don't have to call it nature, or we don't have to call it radical political. We can say what it was, and that is a relief.

MOYERS: The public rhetoric has been filled with race and white and black, and so that it seems a surprise to hear someone say, "Well, now, at least, we can discuss those in literature." You're saying that they weren't a part of our tradition of storytelling, novels?

MORRISON: Oh, no. Not in the critique, not in the discourse, not in the reviews, not in the scholarship around these works. That was not a subject to be discussed. It was not worthy of discussion. Not only that, it admitted that the master narrative could not encompass all these things. The silence was absolutely important, the silence of the black person.

MOYERS: The silence, you mean that his voice, her voice was never heard?

MORRISON: His presence, never heard, and that they don't speak in the text themselves. They are not permitted to say things. So that the academy or the history can't really permit them to be center stage in the discourse of the text, in art, in literature. But in public discourse, when we talk about neighborhoods or policy or schools or welfare or practically anything, the real subject is race, or is class. I mean, that's what it's about. We may call it disadvantaged or undeveloped or remedial or, you know, all these sort of euphemisms for poor people and/or black people and/or any non-white person in this country. That is the subject of practically all of the political discourse there is, but it has been kept out of the art world. There is a wonderful collection of paintings, *The Image of the Black in the Western World*. No one thinks of Hogarth, for example, as having painted all these black people. Or no one thinks of all of the importance, the changes, that the iconography of black people went through. They're everywhere. The country, particularly this one, is seething with the presence of black people. But there had—it was necessary to deny in critical language that presence when we discussed it. I read all those books in graduate school, as everybody did. We never talked about what was really going on. We talked about Huck Finn and Jim, and we'd think about how wonderful the innocence of this sort of radical child is, kind of a paradigm for the American as he comes of age, his generosity—

MOYERS: The white American.

MORRISON: —the white American, because it is about the construction of a white male. But what's serviceable to him, to Huck, is this grown-up black man who is never called a man, who is the battle plain or the arena through which Huck can become a moral person. He becomes a moral person because of his association with this black man who is never called a man. And to Mark Twain's credit, he provides an extraordinary scene where you realize that Jim has a wife, and has a child, and he's trying to get home. Huck's trying to get to the territory, he's trying to get home. And a terrible little thing happened at that moment when he told his daughter to shut the door and she didn't do it, and he told her again, and she didn't do it. And he got annoyed and he hit her, and then later realizes she was sick, she had spinal meningitis or something, and she had lost her hearing. And he's reflecting on that. And he tells that story to Huck. And suddenly there's this man who has a context.

MOYERS: Mm-hmm. He has a family—

MORRISON: He has a family.

MOYERS: —he has emotions, like—

MORRISON: Emotions. And it's an overwhelming thing for Huck, who can say, interestingly enough, these people think about children the same way we do. It's a revelation.

MOYERS: You were saying earlier, when we were talking before we began the conversation, that in the movie, *Glory*, the only reference that is made to the fact that these black troopers have a family is once, when they're being paid.

MORRISON: Exactly. And they say, "We need the money." I mean, "I have a family." But those men are fighting and dying and willing to die for a very important cause, freedom, but it's never contextualized. They're not seen as having children, wives, aunts, mothers. They are a family, that doesn't matter, for whom they are perceived of as not feeling responsibility and who are not responsible to them. And it's so absolutely contrary to the real life of black people for whom the family and the relations are of paramount importance. There is no life outside the family for the traditional black, you know, person.

MOYERS: The artist is supposed to carry our moral imagination. It's astonishing to me that in the 1840s and 1850s, on the eve of the Civil War, in the period of traumatic conflict over abolition and slavery, that the American novelists were not dealing with those issues. Hawthorne was writing European Gothic, with ruins and ghosts, the supernatural. James Fenimore Cooper was writing bestsellers set in primeval forests. The best-selling novels, in fact, on the eve of the Civil War were written—were soppy stories written by women about courageous orphans. Your people never show up in the novels of that time. How do you explain that?

MORRISON: Well, they do. They show up. They're everywhere. They're in Hawthorne's power of blackness. They're in all the dark symbols. They're in the haunting. What's he haunted by? What is the guilt? What is that real sin that is really worrying Hawthorne all his life? They're there.

MOYERS: You think it was?

MORRISON: It's all in Fenimore Cooper. I think it was. I don't care where he took the story. Novelists, writers are informed by the major currents of the world. It's in Melville, it's everywhere in Poe.

MOYERS: But blacks don't emerge as people with—

MORRISON: Oh, no, no, no.

MOYERS: —context, with family—

MORRISON: No. Not three-dimensional. Oh, no. Oh, no.

MOYERS: —with emotions.

MORRISON: No. The characters are discredited and ridiculed and perjured. But the idea of those characters, the construction of them as an outside representation of anarchy, collapse, illicit sexuality, all of these negative things that are—that they feared are projected onto this presence. So that you'd find these extraordinary gaps and evasions and destabilizations. The chances of getting a truly complex human black person in a book in this country in the 19th century was unlikely. Melville came probably very close, with, you know, sorts of classic complexities, but not real flesh-and-blood people.

MOYERS: They were symbols, again, they were—

MORRISON: Symbols, more, yeah, complicated symbols.

MOYERS: —shadows, shadows on the wall back there, at the rear of his cave.

MORRISON: But he gets into bed with him in the very first scene. Ishmael goes to bed with Queequeg. Each one of those white people in *Moby Dick* has a black brother. They're paired together. Fedallah is the shadow of Ahab. Queequeg is the

shadow of Ishmael. They all have them, and they work together in tandem all through the book. So that what I am
saying is that even though the realistic representation is not
there, the sympathetic one you get, sort of, in—if you can
call it, you know, *Uncle Tom's Cabin*, but the information,
subtextual information, it is powerful, what they are saying,
is all self-reflexive, it's all about the fabrication of a white male
American.

MOYERS: Isn't that tension, the fate of this American experience, I mean, from the beginning, when blacks were the
unacknowledged presence at Philadelphia, when the Consti-
tution was being written—

MORRISON: Mm-hmm, exactly.

MOYERS: —in the constant—well, I think your term for it
is unspeakable—

MORRISON: Things unspoken.

MOYERS: Unspeakable things unspoken. Always we are defining ourselves by the other.

MORRISON: Exactly.

MOYERS: Even when it is not spoken, this deep and psychic
struggle going on to—

MORRISON: Exactly.

MOYERS: —to see and not see the other.

MORRISON: That's right. And it can become truly pathological. Truly crazy.

MOYERS: In what sense?

MORRISON: Well, when you think about the instruction one needs to become a racist, or the instruction one receives to become the victim of racism, it's truly debilitating. I don't mean it's vaguely unsettling. I mean it is—I think it can get to be of clinical proportions. It can—it's as though you—

MOYERS: Requiring the surgery of a civil war to attempt to extricate us.

MORRISON: Exactly. And what it does on a personal level is, you—if someone says to me, you know, "This hand is not your hand, it doesn't belong to you. It's on your body, but it's alien," and I'm convinced. So what I do is, it falls off, right, it atrophies. And I have to figure out something to do with it. It's a true severance of part of myself. It's a true severance of the body politic. You know, racism is not old. I mean, it seems to have been around forever, but, say, a thousand years? The human race is what, four million years old? It's not a fixed star.

MOYERS: The interesting thing is, slavery is older than racism.

MORRISON: Of course.

MOYERS: Yes.

MORRISON: This is why there's a double bind in this country, because you had the twin evils of slavery, which, I don't know, everybody knew something about. Everybody's ancestors knew something about that. But you have the visible other, who cannot disappear, who cannot go past, who cannot – so wherever he is, he is the icon and he is the reminder, not only of slavery, not only of degradation, not only of dishonor, but the associations that are racial. And that persists. That persists.

MOYERS: And you say that it deeply infected the literature of—

MORRISON: Oh, sure.

MOYERS: —of escapism, in a sense, in the 19th century, when these gifted men—and they did produce a wonderful body of work—

MORRISON: Sure.

MOYERS: —were writing wonderfully romantic and I mean Harlequin novels—

MORRISON: No, but—

MOYERS: —they were out there in the imagination, where you weren't.

MORRISON: —no. There was an Eden, and what you needed for that Eden was for it to not be susceptible to corruption, that can't fall. America was, you know, this Eden for everyone. It was beautiful and perceived of, although it wasn't, as uninhabited. I was reading something in Bernard Bailyn, and it said, he bought this—this land was perceived of as being this large uninhabited tract, surrounded by tribes of savages. So we had this uninhabited land.

MOYERS: A void.

MORRISON: A void, right. So that, of course, they had to fill. And when they came, you know, they were, you know, dreamers. And what one has to remember, I think, over and over again is what they were running from.

MOYERS: Which was?

MORRISON: Poverty, humiliation, jail, prostitution. I mean, some of them were nice clerks and so on, but they were—some of them were not even running to freedom. They were running from it, I mean, the license that the Puritans understood as corrupt, they were trying to get it over here so they could be disciplined and contained.

MOYERS: Georgia, like Australia, was settled by—they won't like this down in Georgia, but the fact of history is the fact, it was settled by debtors and ex-prisoners and criminals getting a second start over here.

MORRISON: Yeah. That's right. Now, it could have happened that all those people who came here figured it all out and eventually slavery was of no use economically, perhaps. But to make an American, you had to have all these people from these different classes, different countries, different languages feel close to one another. So what does an Italian peasant have to say to a German burgher, and what does an Irish peasant have to say to a Latvian? You know, really, they tended to balkanize. But what they could all do is not be black. So it is not coincidental that the second thing every immigrant learns when he gets off the boat is that word, "nigger." In that way, he's establishing oneness, solidarity, and union with the country. That is the marker. That's the one.

MOYERS: What kind of need did that meet in the psyche, do you think?

MORRISON: Well, these were people who were frightened. I mean, I would be. You go to a strange country; maybe you have some friends there. You need a job. You've cut your bridges. You've said something's terrible back home. You go and you emigrate, you go someplace else. And it's under duress. You're facing chaos. And when you're facing that chaos you have to name it, or violate it, or control it in some way. So you want to belong to this large idea, you want to belong. And one learns very quickly what to belong to. And you belong to this non-black population, which is everywhere. But it serves. It serves. It has always served economically a lot of forces in this country.

MOYERS: That I can understand, but the failure of the writer to deal – to cross the boundary, to incorporate the other into the novel, is one that I don't understand. Although I don't want to run the risk of trying to read into the past—

MORRISON: No, of course, of course.

MOYERS: —the morays and visions and insights of the moment.

MORRISON: [crosstalk] Of the 20th century. But I think many of them did. I think that book by Willa Cather, although she did it late, it's sort of 1938, 1939, '40, but still, her life, her writing life expanded, you know, earlier than that, of this book, *Safira and the Slave Girl*, I think that is a genuine attempt to talk about power, jealousy, othering, the process of entering the other. In that confrontation she sets up with a white, paralyzed, ill mistress and her young about-to-be-a-woman servant, and her response to that is to fabricate some mystical affair that's not taking place between this girl and her husband, and to invite her own relative down in order to rape and seduce her, and to destroy her. It's a difficult book, it's a problematic book, but this is an instance in which a woman—and the women do it, I think, more easily than the men.

MOYERS: Why?

MORRISON: I don't know. I think they're already othered, maybe.

MOYERS: Yeah.

MORRISON: But when you look at the literature of the women, I mean, Harriet Beecher Stowe, after all, is a woman. So is Cather. Gertrude Stein. I mean, in Carson McCullers and reams of others, they are more likely—and especially Southern women. It's interesting. Flannery O'Connor. I mean, when they do—

MOYERS: Eudora Welty.

MORRISON: —Eudora Welty. There's something—and I know this is going to be a great generalization that's going to be proven fallacious, but it seems to me, in the literature that emerges, in which there's a real place for a complicated—either a complicated black person or a problematized relationship between a white and a black, frequently the people who generate that are women, and unbelievably, many of them have lived in the South. That's interesting to me.

MOYERS: Why a different psyche there?

MORRISON: I think it's the intimacy.

MOYERS: Yeah?

MORRISON: I mean, you know, the intimacy and the distance that is probably—had been historically much more complicated in the South than in the North, where there was a lot of illusion and delusion and evasion, I mean, you know, you could sort of hide behind very virulent racism for a lot in the North because of the way in which it was constructed. In the South, it was almost impossible to do that.

MOYERS: I don't mean this to be a trick question, it just occurs to me, though, is it conceivable that you could write a novel in which blacks are not center stage?

MORRISON: Absolutely.

MOYERS: You think the public would let you, because the expectations are you made such a—you've achieved such fame and made such a contribution by writing about black people in your novels that they now expect you to write about black people.

MORRISON: I will, but I won't identify them as such. That's the difference. There are two moments in *Beloved* in which I tried to do it, in which I set up a situation in which two people are talking, two black people. And some other people enter the scene, and they're never identified as black or white. But the reader knows instantly. Not because I use the traditional language of stereotype. There are two moments, one when Pauldie and Sapphire are walking down the street and he touches her shoulder to lead her off of the sidewalk onto the ground, because three women are walking this way. That's all, but you know who that is. There's another moment when he's sort of in despair, talking to a friend, and a man rides up on a horse and says, "where is, I don't know what her name is, Valerie?" and he calls a woman by her first name. "Doesn't she live around here somewhere?" And you can tell by the reactions of the black men that he is a white man, but I don't have to say it. So my thing that I really want to do and expect to do is to do what you say, but I am not writing about white people. I will be writing about black people. But I won't have to do what they did in all these 19th-century novels. They always had to say it. I mean, you couldn't say, "Jupiter walked in the room," or "Mary." You said "the Negro," "the slave," "the black," the this. You know, it always required its own modifier. You take the modifiers out, you see. If you had—if Willa Cather had entitled her book *Safira and Nancy*, that changes the whole book. I mean, the strategies are different, the power relationships are different. But she said *Safira and the Slave Girl*. She has no first name, you know, in the title.

MOYERS: In fact, as you talk, I remember now, back to my own reading in those periods, that you were always called, "the something."

MORRISON: That's right.

MOYERS: Yeah. There was not a name, there was an object, a noun.

MORRISON: No name, that's right.

MOYERS: "The Negro," "the slave," "the Negress."

MORRISON: That's right. Exactly. That's right. Or "my." I challenged my students last year if they could find a 19th-century novel in which a black male appeared and was called a man, without the possessive pronoun or when he was not in the company of a black female, in which case they were distinguishing gender. Just find one reference in which somebody says black man, and I'll take you to dinner, I said.

MOYERS: Did you have to pay out any—

MORRISON: Uh-uh, not yet.

MOYERS: —you haven't.

MORRISON: Uh-uh. But if I write a book and I can do that, whatever it will mean to people who read it, they won't be confused. That will be part of my job. But can you think what it would mean for me and my relationship to language and to text to be able to do that without having to always explain to the reader the race of the characters. Even if, in my mind, they are all black, or African Americans, or whatever the word is at the time. If I don't have to say that.

MOYERS: [voice-over] From the New York Public Library, this has been a conversation with Toni Morrison. I'm Bill Moyers.

THE SALON
INTERVIEW:
TONI MORRISON

INTERVIEW BY ZIA JAFFREY
SALON
FEBRUARY 3, 1998

I met Toni Morrison at her apartment in SoHo. She hung up my coat and offered me a drink, and we settled in for a conversation. I was immediately aware of the gentleness in that room—her listening presence. Morrison's seventh novel, *Paradise*, had just been published by Knopf, and throughout our talk her phone rang continually with news—from her son, her sister, a friend—of the reviews the book was getting. An unhurried and thoughtful speaker, she took it all in stride. *Paradise*—which opens with the startling sentence "They shoot the white girl first"—involves the murder of several women in the 1970s by a group of black men, intent on preserving the honor of their small Oklahoma town; they see the women as bad, a wayward influence on their moral lives. It's an intense, deeply felt book that easily ranks with her best work.

Toni Morrison was born in Lorain, Ohio, in 1931. She attended Howard University, then received a master's degree in English at Cornell University, where she wrote a thesis on William Faulkner. Her first novel, *The Bluest Eye*, was published in 1969, followed by *Sula* in 1973. Then came *Song of Solomon* (1977), which won the National Book Critics Circle Award for fiction, *Tar Baby* (1981), the play *Dreaming Emmett* (1985), and *Beloved* (1987), which received the Pulitzer in 1988. Her novel Jazz appeared in 1992, and in 1993 Morrison was awarded the Nobel Prize for literature. Last year she was the co-editor, along with Claudia Brodsky Lacour, of a volume called *Birth of a Nation'hood: Gaze, Script, and Spectacle in the O. J. Simpson Case*. An editor at Random House for many years, Morrison now teaches fiction writing at Princeton University.

ZIA JAFFREY: Do you read your reviews?

TONI MORRISON: Oh, yes.

JAFFREY: What did you think of Michiko Kakutani's strongly negative review of *Paradise* in the *New York Times*?

MORRISON: Well, I would imagine there would be some difference of opinion on what the book is like or what it meant. Some people are maybe more invested in reading it from a certain point of view. The daily review in the *New York Times* was extremely unflattering about this book. And I thought, more to the point, it was not well written. The unflattering reviews are painful for short periods of time; the badly written ones are deeply, deeply insulting. That reviewer took no time to really read the book.

JAFFREY: You don't feel you need to protect yourself from listening to critics?

MORRISON: You can't.

JAFFREY: You need to know what's being said?

MORRISON: I know there are authors who find it healthier for them, in their creative process, to just not look at any reviews, or bad reviews, or they have them filtered, because sometimes they are toxic for them. I don't agree with that kind of isolation. I'm very much interested in how African American literature is perceived in this country, and written about, and viewed. It's been a long, hard struggle, and there's a lot of work yet to be done. I'm especially interested in how women's fiction is reviewed and understood. And the best way to do that is to read my own reviews, for reasons that are not about how I write. I mean, it doesn't have anything to do with the work. I'm not entangled at all in shaping my work according to other people's views of how I should have done it, how I succeeded at doing it. So it doesn't have that kind of effect on me at all. But I'm very interested in the responses in general. And there have been some very curious and interesting things in the reviews so far.

JAFFREY: *Paradise* has been called a "feminist novel." Would you agree with that?

MORRISON: Not at all. I would never write any "ist." I don't write "ist" novels.

JAFFREY: Why distance oneself from feminism?

MORRISON: In order to be as free as I possibly can, in my own imagination, I can't take positions that are closed. Everything I've ever done, in the writing world, has been to expand articulation, rather than to close it, to open doors, sometimes, not even closing the book—leaving the endings open for reinterpretation, revisitation, a little ambiguity. I detest and loathe [those categories]. I think it's off-putting to some readers, who may feel that I'm involved in writing some kind of feminist tract. I don't subscribe to patriarchy, and I don't think it should be substituted with matriarchy. I think it's a question of equitable access, and opening doors to all sorts of things.

JAFFREY: Because the book has so many women characters, it's easy to label.

MORRISON: Yes. That doesn't happen with white male writers. No one says Solzhenitsyn is writing only about those Russians, I mean, what is the matter with him? Why doesn't he write about Vermont? If you have a book full of men, and minor female characters—

JAFFREY: No one even notices. No one blinks that Hemingway has this massive problem with women.

MORRISON: No one blinks at all.

JAFFREY: Many of the male characters in *Paradise* have severe problems. I was wondering if you yourself identified with any of them as morally strong characters?

MORRISON: I suppose the one that is closest to my own sensibility about moral problems would be the young minister,

Reverend Maisner. He's struggling mightily with the tenets of his religion, the pressures of the civil rights, the dissolution of the civil rights.

JAFFREY: And he's worried about the young.

MORRISON: And the young. He's very concerned that they're being cut off, at a time when, in fact, he probably was right, there was some high expectations laid out for them, and suddenly there was a silence, and they were cut off.

JAFFREY: He's like Lev in *Anna Karenina*.

MORRISON: Right.

JAFFREY: Struggling with the moral —

MORRISON: He's not positive about all of it, but he wants to open up the discussion. He wants to do this terrible thing, which is listen to the children. Twice it's been mentioned or suggested that *Paradise* will not be well studied, because it's about this unimportant intellectual topic, which is religion.

JAFFREY: *Paradise* has also been called a "difficult" book.

MORRISON: That always strikes me—it makes me breathless—to be told that this is "difficult" writing. That nobody in the schools is going to want to talk about all of these issues that are not going on now.

JAFFREY: Do they say that about Don DeLillo's *Mao II*, because it involves cults?

MORRISON: No, there's a different kind of slant, I think. Different expectations. Different yearnings, I think, for black literature.

JAFFREY: You mean, they want you to step into what they've already heard?

MORRISON: And say, once again, "It's going to be all right, nobody was to blame." And I'm not casting blame. I'm just trying to look at something without blinking, to see what it was like, or it could have been like, and how that had something to do with the way we live now. Novels are always inquiries for me.

JAFFREY: Did you have any relationship to the word "feminism" when you were growing up, or did you have a sense of yourself first as black and then as female?

MORRISON: I think I merged those two words, black and feminist, growing up, because I was surrounded by black women who were very tough and very aggressive and who always assumed they had to work and rear children and manage homes. They had enormously high expectations of their daughters, and cut no quarter with us; it never occurred to me that that was feminist activity. You know, my mother would walk down to a theater in that little town that had just opened, to make sure that they were not segregating the population—black on this side, white on that. And as soon as it opened up, she would go in there first, and see where the usher put her, and look around and complain to someone. That was just daily activity for her, and the men as well. So it never occurred to me that she should withdraw from that kind of confrontation with the world at large. And the fact that she was a woman wouldn't deter her. She was interested in what was going to happen to the children who went to the movies—the black children—and her daughters, as well as her sons. So I was surrounded by people who took both of those roles seriously. Later, it was called "feminist" behavior. I had a lot of trouble with those definitions, early on. And I wrote some articles about that, and I wrote *Sula*, really, based on this theoretically brand-new idea, which was: Women should be friends with one another. And in the community in which I grew up, there were women who would choose the company of a female friend over a man, anytime. They were really "sisters," in that sense.

JAFFREY: Do you keep the company of female writers? Do you find a need for that?

MORRISON: I really have very few friends who are writers. I have some close friends who are writers, but that's because they're such extraordinary people. The writing is almost incidental to the friendship, I think. It was interesting to me that when books by black women first began to be popular, there was a non-articulated, undiscussed, umbrella rule that seemed to operate, which was: Never go into print damning one another. We were obviously free to loathe each other's work. But no one played into the "who is best." There was this marvelous absence of competition among us. And every now and then I'd see a review—a black woman reviewer take another black woman writer, a critic usually, on—but usually it's in that field of cultural criticism. Because it was always understood that this was a plateau that had a lot of space on it.

JAFFREY: Have you noticed a change in the intelligence of the criticism of your books over the years?

MORRISON: I have. Over time, they've become much more intelligent, they've become much more sensitive, they've given up some of the laziness they had before. There was a time when my books, as well as everybody else's books, were viewed as sociological revelations. Is this the best view of the black family, or not? I remember once, in the New Yorker, being reviewed, I think it was *Beloved*, and the reviewer began the review and spent a lot of time talking about Bill Cosby's television show—the kind of black family to be compared with the family in *Beloved*. It was so revolting. And that notion—once I was reviewed in the *New York Review of Books*, with two other black writers. The three of us, who don't write anything alike, were lumped together by color, and then the reviewer ended by deciding which of the three books was the best. And she chose one, which could have been [the best], but the reason it was the best was because it was more like "real" black people. That's really discouraging. So if you have that kind of reduction to the absurd, you just have to keep on trying.

JAFFREY: Do you see a place for gay literature, Indian literature, black literature, black women's literature—in a positive way?

MORRISON: Oh, absolutely. It's changing everything. They may take longer; the marketing shapes how we understand these books. Some Native American writers enjoy being called Native American writers. I had a student who was Native American and I told him, "You're going to have trouble getting this book accepted, because there are no moccasins, there are no tomahawks." And he did. He had enormous trouble. I mean, submissions, I don't even want to repeat the number, but he finally did have this book published, and you know, it's a first novel—it got excellent reviews—but the point was that the rejections, I know, were based on the inability to think of Native Americans, in this particular case, as Americans.

JAFFREY: You teach writing at Princeton. Can writing can be taught?

MORRISON: I think some aspects of writing can be taught. Obviously, you can't expect to teach vision or talent. But you can help with comfort.

JAFFREY: Or confidence?

MORRISON: Well, that I can't do much about. I'm very brutal about that. I just tell them: You have to do this, I don't want to hear whining about how it's so difficult. Oh, I don't tolerate any of that because most of the people who've ever written are under enormous duress, myself being one them. So whining about how they can't get it is ridiculous. What I can do very well is what I used to do, which is edit. I can follow their train of thought, see where their language is going, suggest other avenues. I can do that, and I can do that very well. I like to get in the manuscript.

JAFFREY: How did you juggle being an editor, being a writer and being a mother?

MORRISON: When I look back at those years, when I was going into an office every day, when my children were small, I don't really understand how all that came about. Why was I doing all these things at once? Partly, it was because I felt I was the breadwinner, so I had to do everything that would put me in a position of independence to take care of my family. But the writing was mine, so that I *stole*. I stole away from the world.

JAFFREY: So when did you write?

MORRISON: Very, very early in the morning, before they got up. I'm not very good at night. I don't generate much. But I'm a very early riser, so I did that, and I did it on weekends. In the summers, the kids would go to my parents in Ohio, where my sister lives—my whole family lives out there—so the whole summer was devoted to writing. And that's how I got it done. It seems a little frenetic now, but when I think about the lives normal women live—of doing several things—it's the same. They do anything that they can. They organize it. And you learn how to use time. You don't have to learn how to wash the dishes every time you do that. You already know how to do that. So, while you're doing that, you're thinking. You know, it doesn't take up your whole mind. Or just on the subway. I would solve a lot of literary problems just thinking about a character in that packed train, where you can't do anything anyway. Well, you can read the paper, but you're sort of in there. And then I would think about, well, would she do this? And then sometimes I'd really get something good. By the time I'd arrived at work, I would jot it down so I wouldn't forget. It was a very strong interior life that I developed for the characters, and for myself, because something was always churning. There was no blank time. I don't have to do that anymore. But still, I'm involved in a lot of things, I mean, I don't go out very much.

JAFFREY: Who is Lois? Your book is dedicated to Lois.

MORRISON: My sister. The one who just called. [*Laughter*]

JAFFREY: Who's your editor at Knopf?

MORRISON: I have two editors.

JAFFREY: Erroll McDonald and Sonny Mehta?

MORRISON: Yes. You know, I had an editor, Bob Gottlieb, for all my books through *Beloved*. Then he went to the *New*

Yorker. I had to find an editor. And everybody said, "You don't need one, do you?" And I said, "Yes, because I used to be one. I know the value of a good editor." I mean, somebody just to talk to. Bob was very good at that. I learned a lot, just in the conversations. He's funny, he's literate and really able to tell you things—it's not so much writing in the margins of the manuscript, but . . .

JAFFREY: Macro-thinking?

MORRISON: That's right. And so Sonny followed him at Knopf—whom I like a lot, who is terrifically smart about books and publishing. But he was the president of Knopf. Bob Gottlieb was also the president, but he was the only president that also edited manuscripts, who line-edited. Sonny doesn't do that. I mean, he shouldn't do it. Most presidents don't do it. But I wanted someone who—

JAFFREY: Would have that capacity—

MORRISON: That's right. So they said, "What combination do you want?" Even though Erroll McDonald works at Pantheon.

JAFFREY: So Erroll is your actual editor?

MORRISON: He's my . . . yes. My lines. I have no hesitancy about his abilities at all; he's extremely good, oh man, and he's read everything, he can make connections. And he monitors the book in-house, you know, to see what people are doing—you know, the covers—the fabric and paper and all of that really important stuff. *Jazz* was pretty much complete when I engaged this dual editorship, so he had less to do with that. With *Paradise*, I was able to send him the manuscript, say, when I had 100 pages, and get some feedback on it. So the levels of intensity have been different because I've submitted the manuscript under different circumstances.

JAFFREY: So did he actually line-edit the full manuscript, or is it hands off on the fiction?

MORRISON: What he does is write me long, interesting letters. And the letters contain information about what's strong, what's successful, what troubles him, what stands out as being really awful, that kind of thing. Which is what you want.

JAFFREY: You have stated, I think it was in the *Times*, that there was still work to be done, you realized, on *Paradise*.

MORRISON: I regard them all that way, all those books I've written. Years later, I read them, or read them in public, and say . . .

JAFFREY: "Should have done that . . ."

MORRISON: Or "Should not have done this," or maybe, you know, this line. And it goes on forever.

JAFFREY: In terms of *Paradise*, what is your personal assessment of—

MORRISON: Of what I could have done? I wanted another kind of confrontation with Patricia, the one who kept the genealogies together.

JAFFREY: Yes, which she burns at the end.

MORRISON: And some of those young women. You know, like Anna. She has a confrontation with Reverend Meisner— but you know about her, what they think about her, but she has a very subjective view. She's the daughter of someone whom she felt they despised, so she has an ax to grind. So she's reevaluating everything, and has come to learn some terrible things, she thinks, about this town.

JAFFREY: A friend said to me, "Why don't you ask Toni Morrison what makes her really angry?"

MORRISON: You know, I've lost it [the anger]. It's a very, very strange thing. I was telling someone this summer that I felt some [turning point], and I didn't know what it was, you know. It's because I've lost the anger now—and I'm feeling really sad. And that seemed so sad to me. Really sad to me. Now, I did get angry recently, about this daughter [in the book]. And I hadn't felt that furious about someone who isn't in my personal life. Because I get angry about things, then go on and work. And today I was a little angry about Justina.

JAFFREY: Justina?

MORRISON: Justina was that little girl whose mother helped the lover kill her.

JAFFREY: Oh God. In the *New York Post*, yes.

MORRISON: And the part that reduced me to just smoldering anger was when she says she held her hands, as she was drowning.

JAFFREY: That was just the most horrible detail.

MORRISON: And I dwelt on it, and dwelt on it, until I was in a state. Yes, I really wanted to write about her, the child. So I get enraged about something like that, but generally speaking, I guess it comes with being over 64, you just get sort of melancholy.

JAFFREY: Melancholy—meaning you're resigned, or passive, in your responses?

MORRISON: It's overload. You sort of struggle to do four good things when you're my age, and then not deal. I even tell my students that: four things. Make a difference about something other than yourselves.

JAFFREY: What are those four things?

MORRISON: That I do?

JAFFREY: Let's say, in the last year?

MORRISON: Well, I think the book is one, [my teaching] is another, and the other two, I don't want to talk about.

JAFFREY: Can we talk about O.J. for a second?

MORRISON: [*Laughs*]

JAFFREY: What about this notion of "black irrationality"?

MORRISON: The story of the case is a marketable story. And that story is made up of black irrationality, and black cunning, and black stupidity, and the black predator. That's what the story is about. So if you take black irrationality out of it, you don't have a story. Black men in particular, and black people in general, are supposed to be able to do opposite-ends-of-the-scale things, and we don't have to make sense. We've always been considered to be irrational, emotional, lunatic people. So if you have someone that was accepted in the mainstream world as exactly the opposite of that, the threat that one may fall back into chaos is always there. That's not just in this case. It was just played out theatrically, although it's true in almost everything—narratives, stories, about black men in particular. So what concerned me was not even what my little hunches were . . .

JAFFREY: But your hunches, you have written, were that he was innocent.

MORRISON: Absolutely. I have never been more convinced of anything than that, precisely because of "motive" and "opportunity." Forty minutes.

JAFFREY: Forty minutes. You mean, how could it be done in that short a time?

MORRISON: Well, I'm sure that, scientifically, it could be done, but it is truly irrational. Truly almost impossible.

JAFFREY: Physically impossible?

MORRISON: It's not impossible.

JAFFREY: You mean there had to have been two people, or something like that? What is your theory?

MORRISON: I have no theories.

JAFFREY: He had these dream-team lawyers, and they never even bothered to—

MORRISON: No. They decided to just get him off, and not produce an alternate—a television show would have found the guilty party. But that's not the way the legal system works. But the rest of it is, you know—there was a lot of money involved in that case. People got jobs, whole industries started up. Every issue surfaced in it. I think sometime we'll know a lot about it.

JAFFREY: The kids—I don't understand how they heard nothing.

MORRISON: They heard their mother crying.

JAFFREY: But then they heard nothing afterwards, with this violent thing, and the dog barking . . .

MORRISON: No, it's a very intricate, strange case. He's not very helpful himself either, in clarifying much. But my feeling about it was sort of like . . . you know, like when prostitutes can't be raped in court, because, well, they're prostitutes. It's that kind of thing. If you're going to be specific, and try to find out if someone did this thing, that's what you ought to do. Part of the reason that the truth never emerged was not just the success of the defense team, but the media's layering on. All these other issues were layered into this.

JAFFREY: Here's a different question: Whose work, among contemporary authors, do you rush out and read?

MORRISON: Hmm. I follow Márquez. I read anything by Márquez. Peter Carey is someone I've read off and on, but now I've become devoted to. I read Pynchon. I buy those books, list price. And who else? Jamaica Kincaid has a new book out that I haven't read. I love her work. I relish her work. It is incisive and beautiful at the same time.

JAFFREY: Do you want to get remarried? I mean, did your marriage change your thinking about the notion of marriage?

MORRISON: No, I like marriage. The idea. I think it's better to have both parents totally there, and delivering something for the children. Where it's not preferable is if that's all there is, if it's just a mother and a father. That's an isolated horror. I would much rather have a large—a connection—with all of the members of the family, rather than . . . Because, usually, marriage, you think, that little atomic family, which I deplore. But I learned a lot in marriage, in divorce. I think women do. They don't know that they do. I remember sitting around with some friends, all of them who had either been divorced, or separated, or on second or third marriages, had had that in their lives—some collapsed affair. And I said, "You know, I suspect that we all talk about that as a failure. But I want you to tell me, 'What did you learn? Wasn't there something really valuable in the collapse of that relationship?'" And they began to think, and I did too; and they said extraordinary things. One woman said, "I learned how to talk. For the first time, I learned to talk." And another woman said, "I learned high organizational skills. See, I was a mess, as a young woman, you know, keeping house," and her husband was worse. So, to stay in the house together, she had to really get it together. The skills that she now uses all the time. So I said, you know, we should stop thinking about these encounters—however long they are, because they do not last—as failures. When they're just other things. You take something from it.

JAFFREY: What, for you, was a lesson?

MORRISON: I learned an enormous amount of self-esteem. Even though the collapse of the relationship suggested the opposite. For me, I just had to stand up. When I wanted a raise, in my employment world. They would give me a little woman's raise, and I would say, "No. This is really low." And they would say, "But . . ." And I would say, "No, you don't understand. You're the head of the household. You know what you want. That's what I want. I want that." I am on serious business now. This is not girl-playing. This is not wife-playing. This is serious business. I am the head of a household, and I must work to pay for my children.

You can't always explain [divorce] to the children. My children were, you know, accusatory. They were teenagers. Now, of course, they're delightful people, whom I would love even if they weren't my children. But when they were young, 5 and 6, they didn't understand what this was about. And I never, never, ever spoke ill of their father, ever, because that was their relationship. And I wouldn't do that. You know, maybe I was wrong. I didn't want to put that burden on them. I didn't want them to choose.

JAFFREY: When raising your sons, did you try to protect them or guide them through the racial issues that they would encounter?

MORRISON: No, I failed at that. Miserably, in fact. One of my kids was born in 1968. I thought they were not going to ever have the experiences that I had. I mean, there were going to be political difficulties, obviously, the haves and the have-nots, and so on. But they were never going to have that level of hatred and contempt that my brothers and my sister and myself were exposed to. Or, worse, my mother. Or worse, her mother. That it was all getting better. Not perfect, and not even good, but that at some level they wouldn't have that. I was dead wrong.

JAFFREY: Because the 1980s came along . . .

MORRISON: And black boys became criminalized. So I was in constant dread for their lives, because they were targets everywhere. They still are. I mean, if you can find police still saying they thought a candy bar was a gun, or they thought whatever they thought—things that would never be coherent if they had shot a white kid in the back. Could they tell those parents, "It looked like a gun to me, but it was a Mars bar"? It's just surreal. So that is what they are prey to. And I just couldn't fathom it, for years and years and years. That it was *that* bad. I knew it was really bad, but I didn't know it was that bad.

JAFFREY: Did either of your sons go to Howard, where you went?

MORRISON: One did go to Howard. In architecture. Didn't like it. Thought it was not the best place for that. It was a personal decision about the school of architecture. But they were not averse to going to places like that . . . Unlike me, they were focused on where's the best school for what they wanted to do, rather than on the sociological myths, and so on. I appreciated that. But a very close friend of mine, Angela Davis, has known them since they were children. The kinds of women that I had as very close friends were very independent women, very progressive, so they grew up amongst those kinds of women. So they have a different feeling; they're very sensitive about social change, and so on. But what I didn't know was just how, on a day-to-day basis—step into an elevator, and everyone gets out . . . I just couldn't have imagined. If I had raised them earlier or later, I would have said, "Now look, this is what you do." And I would say things like the things my father would always tell me, "You don't live in that neighborhood."

JAFFREY: You don't live in that neighborhood?

MORRISON: No, you don't live in that imagination of theirs. That's not your home. What they think about you . . .

JAFFREY: The reality that they think you are, you are not.

MORRISON: That's right. You are not.

JAFFREY: He told you that? That's amazing.

MORRISON: He was wonderful. He was very insightful. Go to work, get your money and come home.

JAFFREY: He was a welder, right?

MORRISON: Yes. So . . . That helped me, because I always looked upon the acts of racist exclusion, or insult, as pitiable, from the other person. I never absorbed that. I always thought that there was something deficient—intellectual, emotional—about such people. I still think so, but I didn't communicate it to my children enough. I think they have suffered. And being male, too. They're competitive, they feel it in a different way. Maybe as a woman you get so used to being abused and dissed, that . . .

JAFFREY: You just think, "I'll shut this out."

MORRISON: Right. I'm not even going to deal with that one. But they don't do that.

JAFFREY: They deal with it.

MORRISON: They try. And it causes them, I think, more pain than it did me.

JAFFREY: My stepfather, who is black, recently said he would advise young black men to go into therapy. It's helped him come to terms with prejudice. I thought it was interesting.

MORRISON: That is interesting. Because I used to complain bitterly that psychiatry never considered race. I remember saying that, you know, in the moment when you first realize you're a boy or a girl or your toilet training is this or whatever—all these little things that happen in your childhood— no one ever talks about the moment you found that you were white. Or the moment you found out you were black. That's a profound revelation. The minute you find that out, something happens. You have to renegotiate everything. And it's a profound psychological moment. And it's never talked about, except as paranoia, or some moment of enlightenment. It's just as devastating on white children, I read in those novels all the time. Those moments when you found out you were white. In Lillian Hellman—any of those Southern writers— the moment when black and white children play together, and then there's a moment when that's all over, because they can't socialize together. And then the white child, sometimes it happens with their nurses.

JAFFREY: It's like: I love this person, and then, boom, she's gone.

MORRISON: And now this person is gone. Then you don't trust your instincts. You mean, I loved something unlovable? I loved something that's not really among us? I mean, the trauma of that is interesting to me. And I mentioned it in a lecture once, and some psychiatrists asked me to lecture further on the subject. And I said, "No, you ought to be thinking about it."

JAFFREY: I read recently that you once suffered a terrible house fire. Did you lose manuscripts? What happened?

MORRISON: Oh, I remember that. It was my house up in Rockland County. It was just a routine, stupid Christmas fire, in the fireplace, with the coals and the pines smoldering. The wreaths, you know—the detritus, the dried needles were around on the floor and not swept up. And the fire leaped to one of those and leaped to the couch, where it smoldered, and no one knew. I wasn't there. One of my kids was there. And by the time he got downstairs, it was shooting through the roof. So he called the fire department, but it was a terrible winter, and the water was frozen in the pipes. And I lost . . . I write by hand . . . I was able to save some books, but I had all my manuscripts, notes from old books, in my bedroom on the second floor, in a little trundle underneath the bed, where there was some storage space. It went up first. I said to somebody later, "Why did I think that having those things near me was safer than having them in the basement?"

My manuscripts, I didn't care, I mean, I'm never going to look at that stuff again, so that wasn't the hurtful part to me. They had a value, I think, to my children. As an inheritance. But I know I would never look at that stuff again. I would never look at *The Bluest Eye*—seven versions, in hand, of it—again. So I was not that upset about that. Other people might be interested in that. For me, it was the pictures of my children and of myself. Family. And I have nothing. Everything's gone. So, I'm sorry about my children's report cards, I'm sorry about my jade plants, certain clothes.

I also had first editions of Emily Dickinson, first editions of Faulkner—I mean, all the stuff that you just hang on to. Only about 30 or 40 books, but they were all marked up. I had a Frederick Douglass—not the first edition, but a second edition, done in England. And letters, over the years. Whatever there was is gone. It's just the wrong place to store stuff. No excuses. The house burned. I lost a lot of stuff.

JAFFREY: Have you ever been to Africa?

MORRISON: No.

JAFFREY: Do you have an urge?

MORRISON: A big urge, yes.

JAFFREY: Do you think it's an important journey for black Americans, in general, to make?

MORRISON: I don't know. We romanticize it so much. But maybe so, for that reason. Because we're so easily drawn, you know, into the myth of—whatever—a history—a useful little test story. And I want to go to Senegal, because I've been invited there by Ousmane Sembène, and I'm desperate to go. And now, South Africa, I've gotten a number of invitations there.

JAFFREY: Right at this moment, it's like watching 1776, but with black people deciding.

MORRISON: That's something I'm determined to do, because now, I'm hoping I can really make the trips, you know, that are not research trips or whatever else I've been doing all my life. But you just go, sit there and watch, and look, and talk.

JAFFREY: I was there writing a piece on the Truth and Reconciliation Commission. I was there for the Winnie Mandela hearing. Do you think it's finally shifted so that people can acknowledge that, look, things went horribly wrong with Winnie Mandela, and maybe we ought not to embrace her?

MORRISON: A South African woman, who was very close to Mandela, asked me, "Why do black Americans feel close to her?" And I was quite taken aback by her question, because she was very enabling and ennobling to black women in this country when she came, and she has endured things that are unspeakable. And it was only after that that I began to wonder whether there was some clouding over the eyes—deliberate and willful. It's very difficult among many women here, professionally, to say anything derogatory about Winnie Mandela. Anything. I don't know what I think about her. I have enormous—frankly, enormous—admiration for Winnie Mandela, but it's based on her legendary past. And when she came here and I saw her, she's terrific, she's just magnetic. And then when I hear other kinds of things from Africans, or South Africans in particular, I have to fold that into my equation. So now I am curious, very curious, about what is the truth. I mean, what is the real person?

Of course, Nelson Mandela is, for me, the single statesman in the world. The single statesman, in that literal sense, who is not solving all his problems with guns. It's truly unbelievable. Truly.

NATIONAL VISIONARY LEADERSHIP PROJECT

VIDEO INTERVIEW WITH CAMILLE O. COSBY
NOVEMBER 5, 2004

CAMILLE O. COSBY: Professor Morrison, when and where were you born?

TONI MORRISON: I was born in 1931 in Lorain, Ohio.

COSBY: And what were your forename and surname?

MORRISON: Chloe Wofford.

COSBY: And what are the names of your parents?

MORRISON: Ella Ramah Wofford, and my father's George.

COSBY: How many siblings do you have?

MORRISON: I had two brothers, one sister.

COSBY: Please talk about the history of Lorain and what it was like growing up there in the '30s and '40s.

MORRISON: It was unusual I think because Lorain, Ohio was right next to Oberlin. That part of Ohio was just loaded with abolitionists. Women were able to go to college at Oberlin before everybody else.

The northern part was the industrial, so it was full of people like my parents who came at an early age from the south looking for work and it was industrial. Shipyards, steel mills, all of that kind of thing. Immigrants from all over the world there. So that when I went to school, it was with people who some of them didn't even speak English. First generation immigrants, Mexicans, Black people from the south, and they used to pride themselves of calling themselves the melting pot. It was really like that there.

COSBY: Where were your parents born?

MORRISON: My mother was born in Greenville, Alabama and my father was born in Cartersville, Georgia.

COSBY: Please share a little about your parents' background—why they left the South and what life was like for them before they went to Ohio.

MORRISON: Well, their stories of their childhood are, you know, rather painful. My mother left with her mother and all of her siblings, and there were seven or eight of them. And they left Greenville, Alabama at a crisis moment, when my grandmother said that she couldn't stay there any longer because White boys were circling their farm. And she had a lot of girls. I never quite understood what that meant then. And then later of course, I understood exactly what she meant because her husband, my grandfather, had gone to Birmingham to earn some additional money, which he did by day work but he also played the violin and he earned money that way and sent it back. So she was literally a woman alone with all these children—young children.

So she was frightened. So she got on a train and sent a message to her husband that if he wanted to see them again he would be on such and such a train at such and such a time. [*Both laugh*]

And my mother remembers getting on the train and they couldn't tell anybody—they had to leave in the middle of the night because they were sharecroppers. They didn't let you go anywhere. And they were not sure that their father was on that train and the train pulled out of the station and they were all weeping because he didn't show up. But when they got about sixty miles outside, he showed up. He was sort of in hiding. [*Laughing*]

My father's exit was a little bit different. I didn't know much about it. I just knew he left when he was around fourteen years old and he went to stay with an older brother who was in California, and then eventually made his way toward Ohio.

But I learned later—much, much, later, after he died— that he had witnessed lynchings of people in that town when he was a teenager. Neighbors . . . They were businessmen, who had just been taken out, and . . . whatever . . . and there were three or four, in the matter of eighteen months. So, I guess that was like a sign . . . I mean, you know, he left.

COSBY: Yes.

MORRISON: He left.

COSBY: Yes.

MORRISON: So their recollections were, you know, miserable.

COSBY: I heard you say in an interview that one of your grandparents and a great-grandparent were born into slavery and your grandparent—I think it was your grandfather, is that right?—was ten years old when the Emancipation Proclamation was signed?

MORRISON: Yes.

COSBY: Were your grandparents' and great-grandparents' experiences passed on in your families?

MORRISON: Only that of my grandfather, who you just described, who was probably five when the Emancipation Proclamation came. And the story of the family is that he, as a kid, he'd heard this promise or threat—he didn't know what it was because nobody took the trouble to explain to him what Emancipation Proclamation was, so on that day he hid under the bed because it sounded monstrous to him, and when they dragged him out he said he was frightened because this thing was coming. And it was this, you know, a funny story that everybody told.

The story about him that I like best is his going to school one day to tell the teacher he couldn't come back because he had to work, but his sisters would teach him to read. Because when I knew him, he'd do that all the time—you know, the *Afro American* and the *Pittsburgh Courier* and all those Black newspapers were in our house constantly, and he had this reputation of having read the Bible through, I don't know, x number of times. So he was an avid reader and had relied on his sisters to teach him.

COSBY: But they were older so they were in slavery, as well, is that right?

MORRISON: They had been when they were young, sure.

COSBY: And do you know how they learned to read?

MORRISON: You know, one of the reasons I wrote one of my books, *Beloved*, was because in some places, in some families, in some areas, we skipped that part. We just skipped it. They didn't want to talk about it. They didn't embed it in the poetry and in the songs. There were allusions to it—biblical, religious allusions, but no great details, and a lot of obfuscation as though if they were going to move on, they just had to move on because dwelling there was crippling.

So it's like this big sort of absence. Not in the history, but certainly in the art, of what was actually really going on. You know, when you read slave narratives, as I did, and you can hear the gaps and misinformation there in talking to somebody. "It was terrible, it was terrible. But my master, he was fine!" They don't want to be penalized, you know?

COSBY: It is kind of interesting though—or not so interesting; maybe a little depressing—to know that so many African Americans don't want to deal with the issue of slavery.

MORRISON: They don't. It's either humiliating or they felt there's something crippling about it. My position is entirely the opposite. If you don't understand your past, you can't transcend it, you might repeat it, you don't understand half of your life. Knowledge is what's important, you know? Not the erasure, but the confrontation of it.

COSBY: Did family history influence the degree to which slavery and the legacy of slavery are present in your novels?

MORRISON: Yes. By that time I had written *Tar Baby*, which was a kind of—it's almost pre-slavery. I mean, it touches upon slavery but it's all very magical and mystical and less political in terms of what goes on on the inside. Because I was working with that mythology of the "tar baby," just converting it into something else, and that's a very, very old story, and I assume its origins were African, not American. And so the melding of those stories was interesting to me—how you get, in the mythology, a lot of information that is just unavailable in the history because the history's going to be written by the conquerors, obviously.

But I remember thinking about *Beloved*, *I really don't want to do this.* I really wanted to talk about that incident with a historical figure. But I was really upset because I had to talk about slavery in particular . . . and I didn't want to dredge. Did the same thing I'm accuisng everybody else of, because emotionally it's difficult. So, I did it and it was very, very hard, not so much to find the language for it; that was difficult enough. But for me in the process of writing, it is just not authentic or legitimate enough for me to look at it from the outside. You know, I always tell my students "It's not a 'Black father'—it's *yours*. You know, the one you know? That one."

. . .

COSBY: You've said in the past that your parents had very different views about racism and social conditions and the possibilities for social change. Please describe your parents' different views.

MORRISON: Well, my father was convinced that White people were beyond correction, that as a group that you could not fix them and he was adamant. Now, we lived in a neighborhood in which there were White people all the time. I mean, he was living in that community and working at a steel mill and the shipyards with lots of White people, and was a very well-liked man. So I didn't even know how adamant he was until a little bit later. I noticed he wouldn't let them in his house, but I didn't know why.

COSBY: Of course then you didn't know about the lynchings that he—

MORRISON: I did not know that until after he died. He never talked about that. And he just found them incorrigible. Incorrigible. But he was not a fighting man, not an angry man. You know, he was calm, but he was finished as far as he was concerned.

My mother on the other hand, treated every person she

met as a possible friend. She always assumed the best. One at a time. One at a time. And my mother influenced me more than he did.

Later on as things developed I—I had never been in the South and when I traveled there and began to look at things that were blatant, I could sense his feelings, as a college student and a post-college student, much more than when I was in high school and junior high school and so on. Because it's so physically powerful, the segregation and the demoralization. It's just putting you outside the human race.

COSBY: How did their ideas about race have an impact on you?

MORRISON: I found that I couldn't use blanket hatred. It was just not useful to me, intellectually it wasn't and emotionally. I couldn't even write out of anger. I mean you have to get someplace else. It paralyzes you, in a sense. And I thought, you know, what's interesting about racism is that no matter what African Americans do, somebody will say, "Yes, but you can't do that." And you spend a lot of energy trying to prove that you can. And as soon as you prove that you can do that, they say, "Oh yes, but you can't do this."

And the effect of it is that you don't move. You just sit there and hate White people or hate racism or hate apartheid and all your energy's going there. I don't mean that politically it can't be confronted. I'm talking about creative energy. Suppose we just did our work?

COSBY: And make your statement in your work.

MORRISON: And make your statement in your work—those of us who could . . . So I got out of it imaginatively, certainly. So, I was much more like my mother in that regard in personal relationships. But what was significant is that I could not dredge up a kind of plastered on, invented anger in order to do my work.

COSBY: The concept of community recurs throughout your novels. What kinds of traditions and values characterize the community in which you grew up?

MORRISON: Well, I think I recognized the kind of community I grew up in is the African American community where I lived in Ohio, and, as I told you, the first time I began to travel south, because it was the same language. Even though this was like Black neighborhoods in the '50s in the south, the same menu; the same behavior that they expected of us and the same rights that adults felt that they had over us, which is to say anybody on the street could correct you.

I remember putting on some lipstick when I was fourteen and some woman came up to me and wiped it off.

COSBY: Did you know the woman?

MORRISON: Yes, but you know, she wasn't my mother. [*Laughing*]

COSBY: She was just some woman.

MORRISON: Well she was in the neighborhood, and so I

knew her, but I didn't say "What are you doing? Don't touch me." I just let her take it off and shake her finger at me and send me home.

I knew Black men who may have been rogues, but who if they saw me someplace where I shouldn't be would take me home. They were safety for me. On trains, you know, the porters used to give you extra food and little extra napkins, you know. So I always looked at them as safe. And the same thing that I saw as true on the street among Black people in Lorain, Ohio, was true in the South. I had school friends— say, a White girl whom I went to school with and liked a lot. She was a neighbor. I hadn't seen her in about twenty years and went back and she called my mother by her first name. [*Laughing*] It would never occur to me to call an older woman by her first name. Those little things, you know, that one is aware of as a kind of cultural exchange in a certain kind of currency—it's very conservative, very hierarchical. So I was amused and impressed when my great-grandmother came in to visit us and all these uncles of mine who were sixteen, seventeen, stood up when she walked in the room.

COSBY: This was the great-grandmother who had been enslaved?

MORRISON: Oh, yes. They stood up. She had a cane. She was six feet tall. She walked in the room and I'm a little kid and I see those kids—I don't know, eighteen years old, a sixteen-year-old—they seemed to be to me rough, you know, out there, dangerous. And then this woman walks in the room and they shut up. It was very impressive.

COSBY: What were some of the tangible as well as intangible signs of segregation or racism in Lorain?

MORRISON: Well you know, they never had the laws that they had in other parts of the country. But what they did have were understandings. And I became aware of them when my mother and her brothers were very interested when new places opened up in the town. A new theater. My mother was always on her way to the theater the day it opened.

She would go in Saturday morning, the first day, just to see where the ushers were directing Black people. And she would always deliberately go someplace else. Or she would make us sit in these places where we didn't want to sit because none of our friends were there, right? Just to make sure they weren't going to impose any de facto segregation on us.

Same thing for swimming pools. I remember my uncle going into Eisley's ice-cream store where they had a counter and booths and we all knew we could go in to get ice cream. You could get the ice cream and leave but we thought that maybe you couldn't sit down. So he goes in and orders and he sits down in the booth and there's a little altercation there but I mean . . .

COSBY: But they couldn't actually get rid of him?

MORRISON: They could not.

. . .

COSBY: When you left Lorain in 1949, what university did you attend?

MORRISON: I chose Howard University in Washington, D.C.

COSBY: And earlier you talked about touring the South. Was that when you were with the Howard University Players?

MORRISON: Yes. That was a major and profound part of my education at Howard. I really wanted to be at a Black school because I had never had Black teachers. And I wanted to be around Black intellectuals. I really did. And I remember my mother and father saying, "Well, we have enough money that we can give you one year." One year. And I said, "That's fine." Just one year. And we'll figure out what to do later or maybe I wouldn't have second year. And mind you, it was $35 a quarter.

So, when I went there I found it to be, on the one hand, everything I'd hoped, which was my being with principally Black girls and boys, men and women. And almost completely, totally Black faculty. There were lots of Europeans who were teaching there and Americans as well. But it had that really wonderful comfort zone of being without that little extra stress that's there, that you don't know is there until it disappears.

And I also found it very different from what I'd thought.

COSBY: In what way?

MORRISON: Well, I had never been around what I suppose one calls the Black upper middle class, and they were different.

They had different expectations. I came from a place where merit was prized above everything. The fact that I was an all-A student and on the National Honor Society and so was my sister was like, I was a star. But not having certain kinds of clothes or other accoutrement, you know, or not even knowing the difference between certain kinds of labels . . .

Certain people made fun of other people if you didn't have these things, or you didn't have claims to a professional parent or what have you. I was not terribly bright in these ways, but the first thing I remembered is that people liked mean people in spite of the fact that they were stupid, they were mean, they didn't get good grades. But they had either certain kind of hair or some kind of skin or their father was a lawyer or something, so they got away with it. I was just stunned. [*Laughing*] But it didn't bother me too long because I found the Howard Players.

Two things were happening there. One: We had to read these plays. I mean really read them. Not just the way you read them in an English class. You had to really understand them in order to be able decide what the character—you know, the whole thing.

And we read—which we did not do in the English department at Howard—we read Black authors. We read Langston Hughes, people I didn't even know vaguely, you know. But we never studied them. But they did in the theater department.

Third thing is what got you the part was merit, talent, ability to carry the role. And the people who were popular or sought after or at the top of the heap were the best, the most talented people, and I felt comfortable there.

And every summer some ten or nine or twelve of us, accompanied by faculty members, would travel through the south to campuses, Black campuses, and perform these plays. It was extraordinary. It was really . . . I can't tell you.

COSBY: But you also—now tell me if I am incorrect: You ran for a sorority queen while you were at Howard?

MORRISON: Yes! [*Laughing*] I didn't know what all that was about, you know. I didn't win, I have to tell you. [*Laughing*]

COSBY: Where did you go to earn your masters degree?

MORRISON: Cornell.

COSBY: Then you returned to Howard University to teach. Will you tell us about your particular students who became prominent writers and leaders?

MORRISON: One of the most articulate, provocative students I had was Stokely Carmichael. He was really clever, very smart and fun . . . Claude Brown was a student of mine . . . Amiri Baraka—I don't know, I'm not sure about him. He was on campus, but now you know, people say that I taught them when in fact they were my classmates. You know, I can't tell now. All sorts of people say, "Oh, you taught me." And I'm like, wait a minute, I thought we were in the same class? Because I was a student there and a teacher. So I'm not sure. David Dinkins. He was a student. I mean we were in the same class. He was an older gentleman. He was a veteran.

[*Laughing*]

COSBY: Will you tell us about your transition from an educator to a textbook editor for Random House publishing company?

MORRISON: Well, I was not able to get a job when I left Howard University, went away, separated and had children. But in the meantime I saw this ad in the paper for a textbook editor and I thought, oh, I can do this. So I applied, and it worked out. That was in Syracuse, New York, because they were buying a company, a textbook company called LW Singer. Random House bought it. And they were going to move to New York and so it would only be in Syracuse for a year . . . If they were only going to stay in Syracuse I'm not sure I would have taken the job.

COSBY: How long did you work at Random House altogether?

MORRISON: Altogether I think it was about eighteen or nineteen years. A long time.

COSBY: You edited Middleton Harris's *The Black Book*, a scrapbook of African American history.

MORRISON: Yes, I had an enormous education with that book . . .

By the time I got into publishing, the world was opening up

to a kind of integrated book, plus, I thought there was a market now because of the Civil Rights Movement.

So I had already by that time published a book called *The Bluest Eye*, which sold maybe, you know, fifty or a hundred, two hundred copies. And they only printed fifteen hundred. So I thought well let me decide to do something that is both African American and good and popular.

So I was looking around to find somebody to do this book and I came across Spike Harris. Middleton Harris. And he was a collector. He just had everything. Every newspaper, every button, every book—just everything. And he knew other people who were also collectors. So I called them all together. I mean, they had newspaper articles, old magazines; they had tales, they had stories, and out of that sort of collection of these four people came my notion of putting together this book that was unstructured. You know, it was sort of some music . . . little known things, odd things, newspaper articles . . .

And one of the things that I located in there was this newspaper article about this woman, Margaret Garner, who had killed one child and was trying to kill the others in order that they not be returned to slavery. What was interesting was that I knew there was infanticide in slavery on the ships as well as other places. But what was interesting about that piece was that everybody was stunned because she wasn't crazy. They kept saying, "Well she's very logical; she's very calm." You know, she wasn't a screaming hysterical woman . . . and that attracted me.

COSBY: Yes. Somehow it appears that it would be all right if the person was crazy. But I'm assuming that many of those people were not crazy.

MORRISON: No. Many of those people were not crazy. And many of them just threw those children away. And they were not crazy. Once they knew what it was like—slavery—what they would have to be subjected to, they decided . . . Because I think we forget something about slavery: There was an enormous amount of sexual license. People talk about, well, the money; the economy; the this . . . But you realize if you own a human being, you really own them. You can get them—boys, girls—to do anything you say, on pain of death. That's what it means to own a human being.

COSBY: Will you tell me about your roles as an editor and mentor for other African American writers during your time at Random House?

MORRISON: I was specifically interested in finding African American writers, people that agents didn't even know about or didn't have. So I threw out a net, so to speak, and I got lots of interesting people. Maya Angelou published at Random House, her first books. And when I met her and some of her friends, I got more information about who was doing the work. And once they knew, then other people would come. But I was always on the lookout and located people like Toni Cade Bambara, who was very special. And I published the first, I think probably the only, book that Lucille Clifton did that was in prose. She did this book *Generations*, about her family.

And I did publish Angela Davis. It was a big thrill for me just to know her and meet her and work with her on that book.

I published Huey Newton, his collection. I published Muhammad Ali. I published the ones that you would expect that I would vie for and the company wanted me to publish. But finding Gayl Jones, for example, Henry Dumas—Eugene Redmond brought him to me and I just saw this stuff. It was just incredible.

So yes, I was working very hard to find writers.

COSBY: No resistance from your bosses?

MORRISON: Some. Some. But they gave me a lot of slack until they realized that the market wasn't quite there with some authors, like Leon Forrest. I published three books by Leon Forrest and they're beautiful, powerful books, but very difficult books. And so even though he'd had the support of academics, and I think even Ralph Ellison gave him a very strong recommendation, the sales were very low. Now *that* they did not let me keep on publishing—books that weren't making any money. Although at one time in publishing you could do that . . . They decided that they had to make some money, you know, as all those publishers eventually did. You can see the consequences of it now.

.   .   .

COSBY: What are some of the challenges that are specific to being a woman writer?

MORRISON: Well, you know, you're not really in the big leagues if you're a woman writer. Notwithstanding Black woman writers; *any* woman writer. There's something called women's fiction. There used to be. In critical terms, that was always difficult to break out of. I mean, people pay lip service to it but you're never really sure . . . The very popular, very powerful and very good male writers really are the alphas of the writing world. It's changing slowly, but you always understood that you were coming from a smaller space.

COSBY: And so many Black writers or artists don't want to be known as Black this or Black that. And you embrace that.

MORRISON: Yes.

COSBY: Both Black and woman.

MORRISON: That's right. In order to change the labels. No, don't move me out of that category and say that I don't belong; I'm too good to be—as a matter of fact, earlier criticism that I remember distinctly, people—White critics, women— said "She's too good to limit her canvas to just Black folks. If she's going to really be competitive, she has to move out of that very small area." So that just angered me so completely, you know.

COSBY: If it's White, it's broader.

MORRISON: That's right. That's what it meant. That's what it meant.

COSBY: You'd said that in the past African American writers wrote for White audiences, but that you write for readers like yourself, for Black people. How do you address your audience differently than African American writers who wrote for White audience?

MORRISON: It's a very nuanced thing. The assumption is in the language. There's a little extra editorializing where the writer who understands the major readers to be White people has to explain stuff that he wouldn't have to explain to me because I would know.

So you can feel the little explanations. You feel it in Richard Wright . . . you feel it even in Jimmy Baldwin. You know, there's this little . . . editorial work going on. There is none in Jean Toomer's *Cane*. You don't feel that explanatory—

COSBY: Or the obligation to explain.

MORRISON: —the obligation, yes, to make it clear. And the other thing is a kind of address. One of the most important books probably written in the United States is Ellison's *Invisible Man*. There's no question about that. But think of what that title is: *Invisible Man*. Accurate, but he's talking about invisible to them, to White people. Not to Black people.

That's a real confrontation and it's extremely important what he did, but that was just a very theatrical version of what I meant by re-addressing this to another. Assume the reader knows as much about it as I do. As a matter of fact, I used to get some complaints, although they were mixed with praise, particularly from young Black women, about *The Bluest Eye*. They would say, you know, "I really and truly loved that book but I was very angry with you for exposing us." And I would say, "Well how could I move you if I didn't tell the truth?" I don't have to apologize for our humanity.

The point is that we're these interesting people who've triumphed in extraordinary ways. I dare anybody to go through centuries and centuries and centuries of this in this place. We should all be dead. This is an incredible story, not just of survival but of thriving. Think what it might have been like if we didn't have to do any of that since what is a consequence is this extraordinary culture, which is indigenous; it's new world culture that we have made in this country.

COSBY: And it's amazing that we have traveled this far.

MORRISON: Of course. It's a stunning story.

. . .

COSBY: *Song of Solomon* is so rich in folkloric, mythic, biblical and supernatural imagery. Will you talk about some of your sources for this text and the effect of juxtaposing, for example, biblical imagery with an African folktale?

MORRISON: I thought that one of the reasons that writing out of, and within, African American culture was precisely this load of information from everywhere. In my own family, the mixture in the language, there was street language; there was sermonic language. You know people actually quoted the

Bible to you as a child, they had biblical phrases in regular conversation. Or they had lyrics from songs . . . My mother sang like a dream. She just had the best voice that ever was . . . And she sang all day. I mean, there was a time when people used to walk around singing, you know, before radios and before television. Just walk up and down the street, you hear people singing. Or in the backyard or in the kitchen. And that was not just my mother. My aunts, all of them.

Now that quality of richness, when I began to write something like *Song of Solomon* and I was trying to pull from the kind of culture that existed already in a northern town . . . the history was in their songs and the history was also in the little tales they told themselves.

And notice that book stops in 1963. I wanted to get it just before things broke out and became much more articulate and focused, you know, along with the Civil Rights movement. But up until that time that's where that information was coming from.

. . .

MORRISON: Remember I told you about this great-grandmother of mine? She was really, really Black. Very Black. Black-skinned. Really tall and really mean. [*Laughing*] But she was something to be adored. People used to come to her for advice from—she lived in Michigan—from all over the state. And this woman said to us, and her own daughter, that we had all been "tampered with" because our skin was not Black like hers. She said the race has been "tampered with." You are no longer pure. That was very hurtful.

COSBY: She used the word "tampered"?

MORRISON: She said "tampered with." You'd been "sullied" and so forth. Meaning she was not. So that was when I was a young girl. When I went to Howard and I saw this reverse skin stuff, in my mind was this woman who was the baddest thing I knew who said that the color of my skin was less than pure.

So anyway, when I was doing *Paradise* and I read this story in a newspaper about these slaves who had gone to one of these towns and been turned away, I started reading more of those newspapers. They had newspapers all over Oklahoma—"Come. Come. New territory. Settle here." And then I looked at the pictures of the founders. They were all light-skinned men and this particular group had walked this long distance to get into this town were turned away because they didn't have any money, really. They didn't want to take on somebody they had to feed. And it was interesting because this was at the time when everybody was saying, "Oh, welfare's terrible. All the Black people are on welfare," and so on. I said, "Oh, Lord." So I made them all Black and pure. I just changed that a little bit and made them very proud, very pure and maintaining their purity and superceding all these other people who were told that they couldn't get in . . . which is the nature of Paradise, you know what I mean? If anybody can get in it's not paradise, right?

But that worked well for me in order to say something about that historical period and the resistance, which I continued a little bit in *Love*—the resistance of certain kinds of African Americans to any kind of progress.

. . .

COSBY: When did you feel more confident about your color?

MORRISON: I'm still not.

COSBY: Not yet?

MORRISON: Well you know what? The only person that I knew who felt this way—same way I do—is Toni Cade Bambara. She was my friend and I told her this and she said, "You know, I always am surprised at pictures of myself," she said, "because I think I'm darker than that." And I do, too. When I see pictures of myself on the backs of books and things [*Laughing*] I always say why is she so White?

COSBY: Your great-grandmother's words are powerful.

MORRISON: And more powerful now, because you know what? I have been running around all my life saying that I have no White blood. Because the non-Black blood in me is Indian—my mother's grandmother was an Indian lady. Anyway, then my son calls me up and says, "What about that man whose name was Morgan?" which is my father's mother's maiden name. "Who was this White man?" And I said, "What are you talking about?" I said, "There are no White men in our family." So he tells me I'm losing my mind. I'm 73; I'm not responsible, right? So I call up my sister who remembers everything and sure enough. There was this

Reverend Morgan. He was a preacher. A White man who married Carrie and had ten children.

COSBY: Carrie is a Black woman?

MORRISON: Um-hmm. Married. Ten children. Five girls; five boys, out of which come these Morgans and the Walkers. So, this just happened like two weeks ago.

I don't know how I missed it because I think I just erased it. [*Laughing*] Racism is terrible, I mean you just can't even work your way through it while you're working your way through it. I'm working my way through it. I'm working my way through it and then up comes something I realize I had invented this fabricated story about no White blood in my family.

COSBY: Thank goodness your son enlightened you.

MORRISON: I know. He remembered.

TONI MORRISON'S HAUNTING RESONANCE

INTERVIEW WITH CHRISTOPHER BOLLEN
INTERVIEW MAGAZINE
MARCH 2012

We are unaccustomed to artistic or social revolutionaries receiving high honors during their lifetimes. Usually, America's regard for its cultural innovators is, at best, a backward glance. Thus the legion of prizes that have been bestowed upon Toni Morrison might lead one to suspect that she chronicles the preferred version of American events rather than the darker, harder stories of who we are. Among the awards received by the 81-year-old writer from Lorain, Ohio, are the 1988 Pulitzer Prize, and, in 1993, she was the first black woman to receive the Nobel Prize in Literature. Moreover, the breathless veneration put forth by her fans—who include Barack Obama and Oprah Winfrey—might indicate that Morrison is too mired in the establishment for her novels to provoke or critique. All of these assumptions are dead wrong. The author's journey through the literary landscape has always been one of defiance. Ever since her first novel, *The Bluest Eye*, was published in 1970, when the then-39-year-old Morrison was a single mother living in Queens raising two boys and working as a senior editor at Random House, her fiction has remained both unflinchingly visceral and almost biblical in proportion. Her language can be spare, but every color, description, and emotional or collective massacre has a haunting resonance.

It goes without saying that Morrison's literature tackles the national themes of racism and sexism, but her work also resists many of the pervasive liberal dogmas of her time,

particularly the black movement's interest in only present-
ing positive portrayals of black characters and second-wave
feminism's tendency to diminish the significance of mother-
hood—that topic being a clear set piece of her 1987 master-
work *Beloved*.

It is one kind of bravery to refuse to write under the
paradigm of the white-master narrative, but it is quite another kind of bravery to not defect to the most obvious and
immediate rival. In her latest novel, *Home* (Knopf), out this
month, Morrison tells the story of a recently returned Korean
War veteran named Frank Money, who journeys from a hos-
pital in Seattle all the way to Georgia to save his younger sister Cee before she dies at the hands of a white doctor's brutal
medical experimentation. Along the way, Frank discovers a
1950s America that's violent, deeply segregated, and occasion-
ally capable of small measures of generosity, hope, and home.

On a warm spring morning in March, I drove to Morrison's home two hours north of New York City. Her house sits
on the banks of the Hudson River with a sweeping eastern
view that includes a low gray cantilever bridge. Morrison left
her teaching position at Princeton University in 2006 and
moved out of New Jersey in 2011, and this riverfront house
serves as her primary residence. The sunlit interior has a few
of her well-known and not-so-known prizes on display—her
Nobel diploma lies open on a table, while framed on a wall
near the bathroom is a letter written by Antonia Fraser from
her and her husband, Harold Pinter, congratulating Morrison on *Beloved* and mentioning that the novel's sadness
"ruined our weekend."

Morrison wore a two-toned gray sweater, and a purple

handkerchief was wrapped around her famous gray hair. She has the kind of striking bone structure of a face that they don't often make anymore—strong and sharp and perfectly fitting for a future postage stamp. Her voice has such a potent timbre that she could have read me my rental car contract and it would have sounded momentous. But here's the thing: What Morrison says is momentous. She has earned her reputation, the awards, and the mainstream podium. But the podium isn't the message. It's still the words that matter.

CHRISTOPHER BOLLEN: What bridge is that?

TONI MORRISON: The Tappan Zee. They keep threatening to tear it down and put up another one. You know, they wiped out half of Nyack to build that in the 1950s. They compromised the bridge and made it low, probably so it wouldn't destroy the so-called view. The problem is when people commit suicide off that bridge—which they do a lot—they often don't die, they just break their backs.

BOLLEN: Because it's so low?

MORRISON: Because it's so low. They've installed little phones there now, so if you see a car parked in the center with nobody in it . . .

BOLLEN: I read that at the Golden Gate Bridge, which is the bridge most frequented by jumpers, most suicides face the city and not the ocean when they die. Isn't that strange? You'd think they'd face the open waters and not the crowded coast.

MORRISON: Goodness.

BOLLEN: You wrote your graduate school thesis on the theme of suicide in Virginia Woolf, didn't you?

MORRISON: I wrote on Woolf and Faulkner. I read a lot of Faulkner then. You might not know this, but in the '50s, American literature was new. It was renegade. English literature was English. So there were these avant-garde professors making American literature a big deal. That tickles me now.

BOLLEN: At that time did they teach any African American writers?

MORRISON: They didn't teach African American writers even at African American schools! I went to Howard University. I remember asking if I could write a paper on black people in Shakespeare. [*Laughs*] The teacher was so annoyed! He said, "What?!" He thought it was a low-class subject. He said, "No, no, we're not doing that. That's too minor—it's nothing."

BOLLEN: You recently wrote a play based on the character of Desdemona from *Othello*, and you made a point that I had never considered before: Desdemona was raised by her nurse Barbary, so, in a sense, Desdemona does have a background of blackness even before she marries *Othello*. That changes the story of *Othello* quite a bit in terms of what Desdemona was thinking and how she came to understand her place.

MORRISON: And who she would not be alarmed by. I was at

a dinner in Venice some years ago with the sponsors of the Biennale, and one guy said to me, "You know, we don't have that race problem in Europe." I think I might have been tired. I shouldn't have done this, but I said, "No, you threw all of your trash over to us." Peter Sellars [theater director] was sitting across from me and his eyes went big. At the dinner, they had these fabulous tapestries on the walls, and there was one with a big, black king-like figure. Back then, the problems were with class—a Moor could come to Venice and it wasn't a problem. But I was starting to think about that play then. When Peter was at Princeton, he said he would never do *Othello*. He said it was too thin. And I said, "No, you're talking about the performances, not the play. The play is really interesting."

BOLLEN: How did you pick 1950s America as the setting for your new novel?

MORRISON: I was generally interested in taking the fluff and the veil and the flowers away from the '50s. *Was that what it was really like?* I thought. I mean, that was my time. I'm 81. So that was when I was a young, aggressive girl. And it tends to be seen in this Doris Day or *Mad Men*–type of haze.

BOLLEN: A decade done by Douglas Sirk.

MORRISON: Exactly. And I thought, *That's not the case.* Then I thought about what was really going on. What was really going on was the Korean War. It was called a "police action" then—never a war–even though 53,000 soldiers died. And the other thing going on in the '50s was [Joseph] McCarthy. And they were killing black people right and left. In 1955, Emmett Till was killed, and later there was also a lot coming to the surface about medical experimentation. Now, we know about the LSD experiments on soldiers, but there was experimentation with syphilis that was going on with black men at Tuskegee who thought they were receiving health care.

BOLLEN: They were used as guinea pigs.

MORRISON: And that still goes on in Third-World countries. But it was those four events that seemed to me to be among the seeds that produced the '60s and '70s. I wanted to look at that, so I chose a man who had been in Korea who was suffering from shell shock. He goes on this journey—reluctantly. He didn't want to go back to Georgia, where he was from. Georgia was like another battlefield for him.

BOLLEN: The book starts out in Seattle. To be honest, I guess I always think of segregation and race problems as a North-versus-South divide. I never really thought of the discrimination in the Pacific Northwest.

MORRISON: My editor questioned that, too. I did my research. Boeing owned all of that property that's mentioned in the book. There were documents that said, "No Hebraic, Asiatic, Afric, whatever, can rent or buy. They can't live here unless they work as domestics." My editor said, "I didn't know that. We Northerners think of that as always being in the South." I said, "What do you mean, 'We Northerners?'

I'm a Northerner." He said, "Well, I guess I mean, 'We white Northerners.'" Because there is custom—not law, but custom. And then my editor said something about the main character being black, and I said, "How do you know he's black?" He said, "I just know." I said, "How? 'Cause I never said it. I never wrote it. I only describe what's going on. You can't go in this bathroom . . ." Everything is viewed through a screen. The character just deals with the situation and takes it for granted. He's not staging a march because he can't go into a bathroom.

BOLLEN: We have a tendency to romanticize the stability of the '50s in the same way that we romanticize the upheaval of the '60s. You've spoken out about how a certain consumer-friendly, drug-induced version of the '60s has obscured the real social changes that occurred during that decade. Was *Home* your attempt to rewrite the '50s away from the favored version?

MORRISON: Somebody was hiding something—and by somebody, I mean the narrative of the country, which was so aggressively happy. Postwar, everybody was making money, and the comedies were wonderful . . . And I kept thinking, That kind of insistence, there's something fake about it. So I began to think about what it was like for me, my perception at that time, and then I began to realize that I didn't know as much as I thought. The more one looks, the more that is revealed that's not so complimentary. I guess every nation does it, but there's an effort to clean up everything. It's like a human life—"I want to think well of myself!" But that's only possible when you recognize failings and the injuries that you've either caused or that have been caused to you. Then you can think well of yourself because you survived them, confronted them, dealt with them, whatever. But you can't just leap into self-esteem. Every nation teaches its children to love the nation. I understand that. But that doesn't mean you can gloss over facts. I was an editor in the school department of [publisher] LW Singer Co. for a year before I came to Random House. I edited 10th- to 12th-grade literature books. For Texas books, we were forbidden to say "Civil War" in the text. We had to write "war between the States." And of course we had to take out all sorts of words that Whitman wrote. There were caveats, constantly, when you sold textbooks to Texas. And they're still doing it, just with religion. I understand they've taken the word *slavery* out and replaced it with something to do with trade . . .

BOLLEN: Obviously, the interest is not to educate, it's to re-educate.

MORRISON: Another reason for *Home* is that I got very interested in the idea of when a man's relationship with a woman is pure—unsullied, not fraught. If it's his relationship with his mother or his girlfriend or his wife or his daughter, there's always another layer there. The only relationship I thought that would be minus that would be a brother and a sister. It could be masculine and protective without the baggage of sexuality. So the sort of Hansel and Gretel aspect really fascinated me. And his traveling back to save her would be transportation with violence all around him.

BOLLEN: Did you name it *Home* because of that journey back? At the start of the novel, there is a whole section about how the Money family originally lives in a small Texas town and is given 24 hours to pick up and leave their land or else they will be killed. What does home mean after that kind of exile?

MORRISON: It was a regular thing. I have an interesting book that looked at the counties that were "cleansed." A lot were in Texas. It was like the Palestinians. They'd just say, "Go," and if you didn't, you'd get killed. There was a migration—a forced migration. But the naming of the book, well, I'm really awful with titles.

BOLLEN: Hold on. Your titles are great. They have a very pure, singular, uncongested sensibility. Although it's a lot to promise when naming a novel *Home*.

MORRISON: When I was working on the book, I called it "Frank Money." It was my editor who suggested the change. When I wrote *Song of Solomon*, I called it something else. John Gardner [novelist] made me take that title. Somebody said "*Song of Solomon*," and I said, "That's terrible!" I was up in Knopf's offices. John Gardner was up there, and he said, "*Song of Solomon*, that's a lovely title! Keep it!" I said, "You sure?" He said, "Yes!" And I said, "Okay." Then he left, and I thought, "Why am I paying attention to him? He wrote a book called *The Sunlight Dialogues*. He hasn't had a good title since the beginning of time!" [*Laughs*] But by then, it was too late.

BOLLEN: In a reprint of *Sula*, you wrote a foreword where you describe writing that book under the added pressure of raising two children and also having a full-time job at Random House. You were living in Queens. I feel like today we always glorify the young, just-plucked-from-college writer. But it's much harder to start writing later, in middle age, struggling on a book around a full-time job and family.

MORRISON: I started at 39.

BOLLEN: Do you remember writing in those tougher circumstances as a desperate time or a liberating one in terms of waking every morning to face the blank page?

MORRISON: That was a liberation. There were two areas of total freedom for me. One has to do with my children, because they were the only ones who I knew who were not making insane demands on me. They made certain demands, but they didn't care if I was sexy or hip, or any of those things that seem to factor in how we are judged—or at least how I was judged, as a woman in the publishing industry, by a certain kind of ambition. Other than taking rudimentary care of them, they just wanted me to be honest, and have a sense of humor, and be competent. That was simpler for me. Outside was complicated. But the writing was the real freedom, because nobody told me what to do there. That was my world and my imagination. And all my life it's been that way, even now.

I sometimes get stuck—my son died two years ago. I stopped writing until I began to think, *He would be really put out if he thought that he had caused me to stop.* "Please, Mom, I'm dead, could you keep going . . .?" So when I got to that point, I could finish *Home*. But it's not just liberating. It's an education for me. In *Home*, I wrote from a man's point of view. I had never really done that seriously until *Song of Solomon*. I thought, "What are they really like? What do they really think?" My father had died shortly before, and I remember saying, "I wonder what he knew." And then I just felt relief, that, at some point, I would know, because I'd asked the right questions of him, and that it would come. And in fact it did. I'll tell you what helped: black male writers write about what's important to them or their lives, and what is important to them is the oppressor, the white man, because he's the one making life complicated. Then I noticed that black women never do that. In the '20s, they did, but I mean contemporary—and I wasn't interested in it. Suddenly if you took the gaze of the white male—or even the white female, but certainly the male— out of the world, it was freedom! You could think anything, go anywhere, imagine anything . . . There was no longer the problem of looking through the master's gaze. With that gaze, you're always reacting, proving something. So not having to do that . . . I think one of the reasons I'm so thrilled with writing is because it is an act of reading for me at the same time, which is why my revisions are so sustained. Because I'm reading it. I'm there. Intimacy is extremely important to me and I want it to be extremely important to the readers, too.

BOLLEN: You've described your refusal to write a book that comfortably lets in the white male reader as not providing a "lobby" to your books. What freedom not to be writing and measuring what you write as worthy or marketable or entertaining for a mainstream white audience. It must have been doubly bold because you risked not being published.

MORRISON: Publishing was not on my mind. Long before I was living in Queens, I was teaching down in Washington and was surrounded by some serious writers and poets. They had a little group, and we met once a month and read our stuff. I brought old things I'd written and they would comment. But they wouldn't let you come if you didn't have something to read. I didn't have anything else, so I wrote this little story about a black girl who wanted blue eyes, which is based on an incident that I had witnessed as a kid. And they talked about it, and I liked writing it, and they had such good food at these little meetings! But then I put it aside. Then I came to Syracuse. My younger son was just six months old, and I began to write and add to that story before they got up and after they went to bed just as something to do.

BOLLEN: You famously wake up before dawn to write.

MORRISON: I'm very smart in the morning. And also, those are sort of farmer's hours. I like to be up just before the sun. Anyway, after I finished *The Bluest Eye*, I had sent it out to a number of people, and I got mostly postcards saying, "We pass." But I got one letter—somebody took it seriously and wrote a rejection letter. The editor was a woman.

She said something nice about the language. And then she said, "But it has no beginning, it has no middle, and it has no end." And I just thought, *She's wrong.* But the thrill was having done it. And then [writer] Claude Brown recommended somebody to me at Holt, Rinehart, and Winston. But this was back in the day of the "screw whitey" books. One of the aggressive themes of the "screw whitey" movement was "black is beautiful." I just thought, "What is that about? Who are they talking to? Me? You're going to tell me I'm beautiful?" And I thought, "Wait a minute. Before the guys get on the my-beautiful-black-queen wagon, let me tell you what it used to be like before you started that!" [*Laughs*] You know, what racism does is create self-loathing, and it hurts. It can ruin you.

BOLLEN: So by telling the story of a girl who wants blue eyes and thinks she's ugly, your first novel was really out of step with the whole "black is beautiful" program. Does that mean some of your earliest critics were from the black community?

MORRISON: Yeah, they hated it. The nicest thing I ever heard wasn't from a critic, it was from a student who said, "I liked *The Bluest Eye*, but I was really mad at you for writing it." And I said, "Why?" And she said, "Because now they will know." But most of them were dismissive. I thought that in that milieu, nobody was going to read this. Twelve hundred copies they printed, fifteen hundred. I thought it would be four hundred. Bantam bought the paperback. It was a throwaway book. And then something extraordinary happened. I think it was City College. The book was published in '70, and City College decided that the curriculum for every entering freshman would have to include books by women and books by African Americans, and I was on that list. That meant not just for that class, but many classes thereafter!

BOLLEN: You've been called "the national novelist." You've also been called "the conscience of America." In fact, it's hard to think of another writer, except for Walt Whitman, who has been asked to stand for so much of the national voice. Do you ever feel that distracts you from your own writing? That such extreme success is, in a way, a pigeonhole?

MORRISON: I had a little moment of difficulty after I won the Nobel Prize, but I was already writing *Paradise* [1997], thank god. I didn't have to invent something worthy of the prize. Now I just take the good stuff. I remember a grudge, but I take the good stuff. [*Laughs*]

BOLLEN: There's the romantic vision of the Nobel committee waking American recipients from their early morning sleep with a phone call. Did that happen to you?

MORRISON: No, they changed it. They're much more civilized about it. They announce it when they have figured it out, which is in the middle of the night. So it gets out. But they have decided not to make people crazy and call them up at night, and just do it at a normal time for whatever country

they're in. What happened was a friend of mine, Ruth Sim-
mons, who is now president of Brown, she was still at Princeton then, called me up at about seven o'clock in the morning
and said, "You won the Nobel Prize." And I thought, What?
I thought she was seeing things.

BOLLEN: Did you even know you were in the running?

MORRISON: I really never thought about it. So I hung up on
her! I said, "What is she talking about?" Because I thought,
How would she know something that I wouldn't know? She
called me right back and said, "What's the matter with you?"
I said, "Where'd you hear that?" And she said, "I heard it from
Bryant Gumbel on the *Today* show." So then I had to think,
Well . . . Maybe? But there had been so many moments—as
I later learned, more than I thought—when people believed
they were going to get it, and journalists were beginning to
circle, and they didn't get it.

BOLLEN: I think that happened to poor Norman Mailer.
Friends even told him that he got it and he might have given
an interview. But he never received it.

MORRISON: I know. It happened to Joyce Carol Oates once!
The journalists were out waiting for her. But I didn't know
what to do! I just went to class, right? And then that after-
noon, around 12:30, I got a telephone call from the Swedish
Academy saying that I had won—at a reasonable time of day.
I still wasn't quite certain. I said, "Would you fax that?"

BOLLEN: You wanted it in writing! [*Laughs*]

MORRISON: That's right! But the event itself was just heaven. It's the best party.

BOLLEN: I saw the recent Fran Lebowitz documentary, *Public Speaking*, by Martin Scorsese, where she talks about going with you and being forced to sit at the kids' table.

MORRISON: [*Laughs*] I know! She was serious. But it was really lovely. It was palatial and grand . . . and a little inconvenient.

BOLLEN: Is it?

MORRISON: I mean, the risers on the stairs—they were so short—I could barely walk down them. But anyway, I thought it was the best time. It was so much fun. Fran said the right thing to me, she said, "This is the first time I've seen pomp with circumstance."

BOLLEN: When you finally quit your editing job to concentrate on writing in 1983, was that a moment where you thought, *Okay, no going back?*

MORRISON: That was different, because I sat out there on that porch when I quit [*Morrison points out the window to her porch over the Hudson River*]. It wasn't as lovely as it is now because the storm knocked it down and I had to have it redone. But I was sitting out there, and I felt afraid, or something jittery. I didn't have a job. Still with kids. It was a strange sort of feeling. And then I thought, *No, what I'm feeling is not anxiety—this is happiness!*

BOLLEN: Relief.

MORRISON: More than relief. I was really happy. Which is to say I guess I hadn't been. I hadn't felt that—it must have been a combination of happiness and something else. And it was then that I wrote *Beloved.* It was all like a flood when I wrote that book.

BOLLEN: How did you find that article about Margaret Garner [the escaped slave who killed her daughter in Cincinnati to avoid her daughter's reenslavement upon capture], which became the basis for the story of *Beloved*?

MORRISON: I was doing *The Black Book* [1974 nonfiction book by Middleton A. Harris and Morrison], and these guys were bringing me all this stuff because I was going to make a whole-earth catalog about black history—the good and the bad. I got old newspapers from a guy who collected them, and I found an article about Margaret Garner. What was interesting to me was that the reporter was really quite shocked that Margaret Garner was not crazy. He kept saying, "She's so calm . . . and she says she'd do it again." So I decided to look into this. It was not uncommon for slave women to do that, but I thought, *Suppose she was rational and there was a reason.* This was also at a time when feminists were very serious and aggressive about not being told that they had to have children. Part of liberation was not being forced into mother-hood. Freedom was not having children, and I thought that, for this woman, it was just the opposite. Freedom for her was having children and being able to control them in some way—that they weren't cubs that somebody could just buy. So, again, it was just the opposite of what was the contem-porary theme at the moment. Those differences were not just about slavery or black and white—although there was some of that—but in the early days, I used to complain bitterly because white feminists were always having very important meetings, but they were leaving their maids behind! [*laughs*]

BOLLEN: Did you feel a real split between white and black feminists?

MORRISON: Womanists is what black feminists used to call themselves. Very much so. They were not the same thing. And also the relationship with men. Historically, black women have always sheltered their men because they were out there, and they were the ones that were most likely to be killed. As a matter of fact, this was an interesting thing for me. When I went into the publishing industry, many women talked about the difficulty they had in persuading their fami-lies to let them go to college. They educated the boys, and the girls had to struggle. It was just the opposite in the African American communities, where you educated the girls and not the boys, because the girls could always go into nurturing professions—teachers, nurses . . . But if you educated your men, they would go into jobs where they would have to be confronted or held down. They could never flourish so easily. Now that has changed in any number of ways, but it was like an organism protecting itself.

BOLLEN: In *Home*, there's the zoot-suited man that haunts the narrative and appears before the main character a few times. How did he enter the novel?

MORRISON: Well, a lot of the book confronts the question of how to be a man, which is really how to be a human, but let's say "man." And he's struggling with that, and there's certain pro forma ways in which you can prove you're a man. War is one. But the zoot-suit guys, postwar, in the late '40s, early '50s, they were outrageous—they were asserting a kind of maleness, and it agitated people. The police used to shoot them. You talk about dress, not to speak of hoodies—they were always arresting those guys. I wanted this figure of a fashion-statement male to just hover there.

BOLLEN: You bring up hoodies. Is there a link between what happened then to what is happening today with the Trayvon Martin case? There was the Million Hoodie March. Do you think situations like Trayvon Martin's shooting still happen all of the time and they just aren't reported? Or have we curtailed the systematic murder of black men in America?

MORRISON: The hoodie is just a distraction. I thought they should have had a Million Doctors March or something like that! For me, it's highly theatricalized now, very theatricalized in the media. The killing of young black men has never changed all that much, with or without hoodies. I don't know of any young black men who haven't been stopped by cops. Ever. My sons . . . I was listening to Jesse Jackson talk about his sons—one was in law school and one was in business school. But they were all stopped. I remember Cornel West telling me he was teaching somewhere and he had to commute. He was stopped every time. It doesn't matter if the car is new or beat up—Cornel's was beat up, they still stopped him. [*Laughs*] So the pervasive notion of black men as "up to no good" may be spoken about more right now in the media, but it's no less pervasive than it's always been. It's like my character Frank Money in *Home*. I just took it for granted that the police would search him on the street. But I'm interested in what the consequences of this situation will be for any number of reasons. There are two things I want to know, and I may spend some time doing research. One is, has any white man in the history of the world ever been convicted of raping a black woman? Ever?

BOLLEN: I can't think of one offhand.

MORRISON: I just want one. The other thing is, has any cop shot a white kid in the back? Ever? I don't know of any. Those are two things I'm looking for. And then I will believe all this stuff. Once I find a cop who shoots a young white kid for being in the wrong place at the wrong time.

BOLLEN: That never seems to happen, does it? Back in 2008, when Barack Obama was running for office, he asked you for an endorsement, which you eventually gave. You said having him in the office would be a restitution. You called it a necessary evolution and not a revolution.

MORRISON: Did I say that? It sounds good! [*Laughs*]

BOLLEN: You did. Now, on the eve of his reelection, do you think Obama fulfilled those expectations?

MORRISON: More. More. He's better than I thought he would be.

BOLLEN: I feel that way overall. There are moments where I've had some doubts, but it's natural to lose confidence with a president at certain points in a presidency.

MORRISON: Of course, but what I didn't expect was the amount of hostility. I knew there would be some—maybe even lots—but this is really deranged. For the people who hate Obama, it doesn't matter what he does. Nothing matters. And the things they say are so retro. I decided that once they have something called the n-word that no one can say, it did the opposite of the word *like*. Taking the n-word—N-I-G-G-E-R—out of language left a hole. So now there is this flood of other words—Kenyan and no-births—that they have produced in order to fill that hole. The n-word used to say it all. Now there's this other loaded vocabulary that's become totally insane. It's the opposite of *like*. As in, "I'm, like, 'Wow . . .'" Or, "It was, like . . ." Or, "I'm thinking, like . . ." *Like* has taken 90 words out of the vocabulary. They don't say *felt* any more. And I get really upset about that. So there's a word that erases language, and then there's the erasure of a word that produces a deranged kind of language. That's startling to me. And the response from the people who dislike Obama is a really visceral dislike. I read a sentence in a newspaper article that said, "The real problem is that here's a black man in charge of the world." It's not a judge or a doctor or the head of a neighborhood—it's the world. Some people aren't able to deal with that.

THE LAST INTERVIEW

ALAINELKANNINTERVIEWS.COM
INTERVIEW WITH ALAIN ELKANN
OCTOBER 14, 2018

Toni Morrison lives in a sun-filled house by the Hudson River. On a Saturday afternoon Victoire Bourgois and I took a ride 45 minutes up the Hudson River with a driver who had lived his whole life in New York and pointed to us all the different areas of New Jersey, Upstate, Yonkers, Connecticut. When we arrived she greeted us warmly, and when talking about her writing process she said: 'My desk does not face the river, otherwise I would not do a thing all day but watch the river. Here there is a mixture of salt water and tidal movements and fresh water, because it is so close to New York City.

ALAIN ELKANN: Have you lived in your home on the Hudson River for many years?

TONI MORRISON: In the county for about 35 years, in this place maybe 15 or 20 years. This house burned down one year, and we all moved to New York City until I rebuilt it.

ELKANN: You worked as a Random House, um—

MORRISON: Editor, yeah.

ELKANN: —editor, in New York City, right? For how many years?

MORRISON: I don't know. I have to tell you something—it's a big secret, but I want you to know. I'm 87. [*Laughing*] So I don't remember anything! [*Still laughing*] But that was good. I liked working at Random House.

But you know I was the only—I think, Doctorow* occupied that place, at one point, the position of being a writer and an editor. And then he decided he didn't want to be an editor anymore, so he quit, and just wrote books. I, on the other hand, didn't have that luxury, since I was raising two sons. So I kept the job. But I was an author and my editor was at Knopf—Bob Gottlieb, whom I just spoke to, he's harassing me about another book. Then of course I was editing other people's work. So to be an author and an editor—I don't know, there was only Doctorow, I think, who did that for about a year. I didn't have any difficulty—

ELKANN: But you left. You left to become a writer. But then you were also a professor at Princeton. You left to become a professor, or you left to become a writer?

MORRISON: No, the writer thing was always with me. I mean, when was *The Bluest Eye*? That was in 1972 or something. So I was always writing, whether I was an editor or not. And then, when I left Random House—or, yeah, Knopf, actually—well I had to have a job. It was necessary for me to have an income. Always.

---

* E. L. Doctorow (1931–2015), the esteemed American novelist who was, for many years, an editor at the New American Library and the Dial Press, where he worked with writers as varied as Ian Fleming and Ayn Rand to James Baldwin and Norman Mailer.

ELKANN: Your books were not selling enough?

MORRISON: They sold well, but, you know, you can't make any money with a novel. No one makes money with a nice novel, or an elegant one. It's usually crime novels and, you know, sex novels, or whatever, for money. The good thing was, whatever they paid me in advance, the sales earned back, so I didn't owe the company money after the book was published—which isn't always the case, you know, with a writer. And sometimes they made money.

ELKANN: But you didn't trust—you wanted another job.

MORRISON: I wanted to write! I *had* another job. I was teaching at Yale, Cornell—at the time that I was an editor at Random House, one day a week I went to teach in a college. And it was interesting because after I started taking Fridays off to go teach, other people in the building, other editors, began to do the same thing. They said well if she can do it, I can do it!

ELKANN: This was around the time when you met Umberto Eco*?

MORRISON: Eco?

ELKANN: This was in the seventies?

---

* Umberto Eco (1932-2016) was an Italian novelist and semiotician who authored numerous books, including *The Name of the Rose* and *Foucault's Pendulum*.

MORRISON: Yeah, yeah, yeah. I met him twice. Once in Italy. Why was I in Italy? I don't know. And then he came to wherever I was teaching, maybe Princeton, just for a couple days.

ELKANN: Your university was Princeton?

MORRISON: Before that it was SUNY, State University of New York, and then I got a call from a woman at Princeton to see if I want to leave the state university and move to Princeton. And my kids were of an age by that time—I had two sons—that I thought needed me.

ELKANN: You've said that you were writing very early in the morning, no?

MORRISON: Yeah.

ELKANN: Because you had the sons.

MORRISON: Because I had to beat my sons. You know, they woke up at, I don't know—As soon as the sun came, whatever season it was, I would wake up in the dark, just before sunrise, because I remember sitting at my desk, looking out for it, and it was always like 15 to 20 minutes before sunrise. But I'm very, very smart in the morning! As the day goes on it just goes away! [*Laughs*]

ELKANN: How many hours did you write? One hour, two hours?

MORRISON: I would write till lunch. But I would get up at 5:30, six o'clock, and I would be finished by the middle of the day.

ELKANN: You've said you were working early in the morning, right?

MORRISON: Yeah, that's what it was.

ELKANN: How long?

MORRISON: I'd start writing early in the morning, when I got up, which was before the sun, because I would always beat the sun. And that would last until lunch. Noon or so. Now that's like six hours, but those six hours were pretty fruitful but, you know, not always. Sometimes you have to just go back over what you already wrote and correct it, or erase, cross it out . . .

ELKANN: Because you were the editor of yourself?

MORRISON: Exactly right. [*Chuckles*]

ELKANN: How is it to be the editor of yourself? Are you more tough with yourself than you are with other writers? You've said that you were writing because you wanted to read what you wrote, right?

MORRISON: Yeah.

ELKANN: So when you read what you wrote, were you as impartial as if it were another person?

MORRISON: Yeah. Another person very like me. [*Laughs*] You know, but I did have to make some boundaries so that I wasn't pleased, perpetually pleased, with everything I wrote. That never happened.

ELKANN: You were not?

MORRISON: No. And sometimes, you know, it's just a mystical thing. I remember a sentence floating around my head for like, a whole summer, and I didn't know what it meant, or why was it staying in my head. And then I sat down and wrote it out on a piece of paper, and after I did that, another sentence came. [*Laughing*] And then another one. You don't know how it's gonna happen.

My desk downstairs faces the—it doesn't face the river, it faces the yard on the edge of the river, because I don't want to look at the river all day or I won't write anything. So I was looking on the side, this way, and a woman came out of the water, and she walked up the edge of the water along my yard, and then she sat down on a rock. And she was fully dressed, she had on a hat and a nice dress, and so on. So anyway, she's in the book, fully dressed, I fit the sentences in there . . .

ELKANN: You wrote longhand, right?

MORRISON: Yes. On yellow tablet paper. Yeah, that's old school. [*Laughs*] That's the way we were taught.

ELKANN: But why with pencil?

MORRISON: Because . . . if you wrote with ink it sounded a little arrogant. Pencil sounded like you knew what you were doing but you were willing to erase.

ELKANN: You wrote many books, right?

MORRISON: Um-hmm. About eight, I think. Some I would like to do over. One I would like to do over.

ELKANN: Which one?

MORRISON: *The Bluest Eye.* The first book. I know more now. I'm smarter.

ELKANN: *The Bluest Eye*—the little girl wants to have blue eyes, right?

MORRISON: Yeah. I liked her a lot, as I was writing about her because she was a real little girl. When I was seven or eight years old I had a friend, a neighboring friend, a girl, who was my age, and we were walking down the street, and she said that every night she prayed—we were having a sort of verbal quarrel about whether or not God existed—

ELKANN: At age seven?

MORRISON: Yeah, because she said there was no God. And I said, *There is a God*, and—whatever. So that's what we were quarreling about. The presence of absence.

ELKANN: And she had no God because she didn't have blue eyes?

MORRISON: Well that's why she *knew* there was no God. Because every night—or every day or morning, every something—she prayed, she spoke to God, and asked for blue eyes, and He never ever delivered. So if He didn't give her blue eyes, the way she asked, obviously, he didn't exist! [*Laughs*]

ELKANN: In your experience, African American people, they don't want to be African Americans, they want to be Norwegians?

MORRISON: No no no, she was beautiful, actually, although I didn't realize it at the time. But she was incredible—she was pitch black, with this incredible beauty—the shape of her head, her lips, her nose, these big eyes—

ELKANN: She was very beautiful?

MORRISON: Gorgeous! But she only was concerned about the color of her skin. And I turned to look, to see, and I thought, *What?* I didn't know *beauty* at that age. And I was sort of struck. That's the first time I looked at a friend, girlfriend, and realized—and thought she was beautiful. That word wasn't in my vocabulary. You know, there was cute, pretty, but beautiful? That was something like the sky, or something. Anyway.

ELKANN: But in your books, you describe the condition of African-American people as difficult, right? But at the same time you have a little nostalgia for the '50s.

MORRISON: Yeah, the difficulty was—

ELKANN: Is it because you were young, or is it because—

MORRISON: No, it was because—no, the difficulty that you reminded me of—of being Black—we were not people, we were *Black* people. Therefore there was this separation. And I don't remember being unhappy, or my friends and family being unhappy about that, but there were certain things we were not able to do, and certain places we were not able to go. You know, restaurants, neighborhoods, and so on. But we made our own neighborhood. For instance, we lived on the shore of Lake Erie and there was a Lake Erie park that the city supported, and no Black people were allowed in there. So what they did—what *we* did—was go further down the shore, about a mile down, and make entrance into Lake Erie there, as opposed to here. We just made our own park.

ELKANN: This was a time where many minorities, even the Jews, were not accepted in society.

MORRISON: No no, they were very isolated. The only difference was, at least for people in my area, whether it was race, or Jews, or Italians—boy, they were mean to Italians!— the group that was acceptable were the sort of middle-class, upper-class whites who lived on the shore. They were doctors and dentists, so they thought they were kings and queens, and everybody else was below them. But uh, I guess it affected grown-ups more than it did the kids because we all went to school together. In my fourth grade, there were two Italian kids who could not speak English, they were fresh off a boat, and my teacher made me sit with them so they could learn to speak English, which I did.

ELKANN: You liked to teach, right?

MORRISON: I liked teaching those little punks. [*Laughs*] I feel smart because he was the mayor of our little town at one point, when he grew up.

ELKANN: You have been a professor for many years.

MORRISON: I love teaching because you learn so much. It's not just me telling them, it's what you get back, which I really like. It's not just me talking, it's the conversation, in a sense. I taught at Princeton for something like seven years. I just left not so long ago. My secretary is still there—Ruth.

ELKANN: Do you prefer teaching to editing?

MORRISON: You know I don't know. I think probably now I would prefer editing. I think. That's because I'm 87 years old and I don't wanna go nowhere. But normally, the two of them are almost the same thing for me.

ELKANN: Do you still write?

MORRISON: "Oh yes," she said. [*Laughs*]

ELKANN: You still write at five in the morning?

MORRISON: No. [*Laughs*]

ELKANN: When do you write?

MORRISON: Right now, you know, now I can't do it. I wake up that same time, but the physical stuff is so different now, you know.

ELKANN: When do you write now?

MORRISON: Hm, night, right now.

ELKANN: In the afternoons?

MORRISON: Later than that, I'd say. Sort of like evenings, six o'clock, seven o'clock. Like that. Yeah. Sometimes it's three pages, you know. Like that yellow paper over there, those tablets. Sometimes I can do three of those. Sometimes I do half of one, you know, depends on—it's not so much the amount as it's what's clear in my mind, what I want to develop.

ELKANN: How does it work, the process of a novel? You are obsessed with one story?

MORRISON: Oh, I don't know, some of it's—it's different—

ELKANN: If you have one book, a new one, you stick with that?

MORRISON: Yeah, just one book.

ELKANN: How long does it take to write a book?

MORRISON: Three years is the shortest time I've spent writing a book. Most of them take six or seven.

ELKANN: Your most famous book is *Beloved*?

MORRISON: I don't know, is it?

ELKANN: [very unclear, 15:05]

MORRISON: I don't know if that's why. I thought it was my other one.

ELKANN: You think it's your best novel?

MORRISON: No.

ELKANN: No?

MORRISON: My best novel is *Jazz*. But nobody cares about it but me. Because I never used the word jazz, but I framed, I designed it the way jazz music is—not produced, but created. It has that quality. You never know—you know, it's inventive, it changes . . .

ELKANN: What is the story about?

MORRISON: I'm not telling you. You won't get that from me. I want *you* to read it. [*Laughs*]

ELKANN: I will read it then.

MORRISON: It's about that period, you know, the 1920s, in a big city like New York.

ELKANN: You do research for that?

MORRISON: I did some on New York, at that time. What the buildings looked like—it was very hip, the '20s in New York City. And the music was great. There wasn't even much segregation. There was a lot of mixture, you know? Because of the music, I think. If you walked down Harlem, Fifth Avenue, you could just—it was lovely. The way other people talk about it, too, makes it sound like *the* most exciting place, and the only one that was close to it was New Orleans. But both of those places, it's occurred to me, are music places. Jazz in New Orleans, musicians living there, playing there. Satchmo* and all those guys. And then New York was a different kind of music—

---

* Satchmo was a nickname of trumpeter Louis Armstrong, who was born in New Orleans.

ELKANN: You love music.

MORRISON: Love it.

ELKANN: Because there is music in your books.

MORRISON: Well that's the only way I could do it, because I can't play it.

ELKANN: And there is always music in your books, no?

MORRISON: Yeah, that makes sense. My mother was one of those people who sang all the time, and with a *beautiful* voice. She never took any lessons, she was just a natural singer. She sang better than anybody I ever heard. Bessie Smith, all those women. Anyway. So she made us take piano lessons, which we thought was like telling us we had to go learn how to walk! [*Laughs*] We had to go to school to learn to do what she did naturally and all the time?

ELKANN: Phillip Roth did not want to be considered a Jewish writer, but a writer.

MORRISON: I remember that. I knew him.

ELKANN: Are you a Black writer, or are you a writer?

MORRISON: I'm a Black writer. No hiding.

ELKANN: Why are you a Black writer?

MORRISON: Because people like you ask the question. [*Chuckles quietly*] It's different.

ELKANN: What's the difference?

MORRISON: The quality, the music, the sound, the texture . . . And what is it about? You know, Black people writing—what was the other one's name? Oh, I can't remember. He came before Baldwin,* and he wrote about Black life but it was sort of distant, as though he looked at it as though it were separate from him. Baldwin wasn't interested in Black anything, he was interested in the craft, and in the world. You know, he lived in Europe, most of the time anyway. But both of those were extremes in their relationship because, you know, if you were a writer and also Black, you *didn't* get reviewed in the *New York Times*. You *didn't* get positions at the universities.

ELKANN: Since then, the world has a lot changed in your lifetime.

MORRISON: A lot changed. Yes it has. Although I have to say, when I won the Prize,† there was some negativity in the press. [*Laughs*]

ELKANN: How was it for you, you know, the Black story in America went through a lot since —

---

* James Baldwin (1924–1987) American novelist, essayist, and short story writer, who authored numerous books including *Notes of a Native Son, The Fire Next Time, Giovanni's Room*, and *Go Tell It on the Mountain.*

† The Nobel Prize, which Morrison won in 1988.

MORRISON: Yeah, yeah, it was a lot of suffering and then people used it in their music, like Nina Simone, you know what I mean? They pulled from it, which is natural. But the writers —

ELKANN: You, too. You used it in *Beloved.*

MORRISON: Yeah. It's there. But it's not confined to Black people. You know, white writers do the same thing. They go into the places that are most hurtful, in their youth or in their neighborhood or in their families, and they pull from that a kind of elegance in terms of their writing. There are very few writers that just write happy stuff. They all think they're Edgar Allen Poe.

ELKANN: So tell me about you and this changing. Because you lived through a very interesting period—right?—of changing for a Black person, vis-à-vis your parents, your grandparents —

MORRISON: Yeah, yeah, big changes . . .

ELKANN: I mean, when Obama became president, what did you feel?

MORRISON: I love Obama. [*Laughs*] That's my feeling. And he loves me! Well, I don't know about that—well yes I do, he invited me to a party. Me, my son Ford and I went.

ELKANN: Do you think this was just one episode?

MORRISON: I wonder.

ELKANN: Do we live in a different America now—again?

MORRISON: Well that's done. There was Martin Luther King, and then there was Obama. *He won twice.* We often elect somebody and then never let them become elected again, you know, they have one term. But he had two terms. His daughter came here once—the older one, I think. She was interested in writing, and uh, I don't think it was him, I think it was his wife who asked me would I talk to her daughter who was interested in becoming a writer. And I said of course. So she came here, in a limousine, and we talked. She was lovely, a lovely girl.

ELKANN: Do you think there is more freedom and less prejudice now?

Morrison: I do. Well, my life has changed because I'm well known. But the real test is that my grandchildren, teenagers, will never think about the things that I thought about at their age. And their mother who, you know, attended Woodrow Wilson College and Princeton, so they're not even in the same category, you know.

ELKANN: Your grandchildren don't feel different?

MORRISON: No, they feel superior. My grandchildren—one is in Jordan at the moment, studying Arabic. Not as a Black girl, but as a person who wants to study Arabic in Jordan, which is like—[*Laughs*] Oh, really? That would never have occurred to me at that age. I was a very proud Black person, like being a very proud, I don't know, gay person. Or, you know—there's always a little category you could put yourself into. Whether it meant anything or not . . .

ELKANN: What does it mean to be a very proud Black person?

MORRISON: Mean? [*Laughs*] My mother was always "better than." She was the best singer, she sang in the church, and her voice was so beautiful that white people came from other parts of the state just to hear her sing. So I had an entirely different perception of what being, oh God, I guess on the edge of society versus on top, meant. But that was in Ohio, that's a different state. That probably wouldn't have happened in Georgia.

ELKANN: Nowadays, the world is going back. Nationalism, fascism is coming back in Europe.

MORRISON: Oh, God!

ELKANN: Do you think America is in danger?

MORRISON: Yes. It's just a kind of a corruption—corruption without embarrassment. I mean, normally when you get a sort of bad leader, whole bunches of people are embarrassed. Now, some people are embarrassed, regardless of race, about Trump. But not enough. I mean, can you imagine—I mean, he lies every minute, everything he says. [*Laughs*]

ELKANN: And he's bad with the Black population, no?

MORRISON: He's okay, the same. He doesn't care. It doesn't matter to him, race.

ELKANN: He is not a racist?

MORRISON: I don't know. But he wouldn't fall into that category—racist—because that's not important to him. Money is important to him. I suppose he likes *rich* Black people.

ELKANN: To be a writer today, in America, is it different? Do people read less?

MORRISON: Well, the response to writing is different because I think people—I don't know, I may be wrong about this, but I taught in universities for so long, so I'm a little bit out of it, but I have a feeling people don't read the way they used to.

ELKANN: They don't?

MORRISON: I think they do not, and they don't read as much, and when they do they don't want to read certain kinds of things, you know? I don't know, I may be a little bit off because I'm not teaching anymore, but when I was at Princeton all those years, I could sort of feel what the atmosphere vis-à-vis important books was. Now that I'm out of there I don't know, I just have to rely on my secretary.

ELKANN: Why do you write?

MORRISON: I'm very good at it. That's one of the reasons. I know how. I always knew how. The problem was that other people didn't think so.

ELKANN: What induced you to write when you were young? Why did you become a writer?

MORRISON: I was in grade school and my mother came to visit the teacher on one of those days where parents come and talk to the teacher about their children. And my teacher told my mother to be very careful with me because I was very talented. And I think I mentioned the little Italian boys that they put next to me so they could learn the language. I remember once, because my maiden name, my last name, was Wofford, and in those days we sat alphabetically. So if your name was a W you'd be in the back, or a Z, or a V, you know, you'd be in the back of the classroom. So I was at the back of the classroom. And a girl named Shirley Vick, V-I-C-K, was sitting next to me. And the other kids were Italians. You just put 'em back there with people like me and Shirley Vick.

ELKANN: How did you start writing? You wrote a short story?

MORRISON: I don't think I did any of that until I went to—I'm remembering—when I went away to college. I don't know what I did in high school. Maybe I wrote something but I don't remember. Because I went back to the university maybe thirty years ago and one of my colleagues was there and I went to see him, and we had coffee—he used something I wrote when I was there in his class as an example of good writing that he gave to all of his students.

ELKANN: What is good writing?

MORRISON: [*Sighs.*] I wish I knew. I can do it, but I can't describe it. [*Laughs*]

ELKANN: Did the Nobel Prize change your life?

MORRISON: No. They gave me some money, which I spent. It made a lot of people mad. They wrote very—not insulting, but close to insulting, articles that were really hurtful. What'd they give it to her for? [*Laughs*]

ELKANN: Once you have so many awards and recognitions, does it become more difficult to write?

MORRISON: No. Look at that. You see that? That's my new novel. I spent the morning talking to my editor about that manuscript. That's called *Justice*.

ELKANN: You like very short titles.

MORRISON: I do, now that you mention it. I hadn't thought about it but it's true. It's just that if it comes that way, it sums up for me something in the book—either a character or a person, somebody who *lives* there, or you know, a kind of atmosphere.

ELKANN: Would you like it to be said that you're poetical?

MORRISON: Some people have said so. I like it, because I know what they mean. They mean it's kind of an elevated language. All novels should be elevated. I don't want, I don't like journalistic prose for a novel.

ELKANN: You have a writer that you really admire?

MORRISON: Caldwell* was a great favorite of mine for years and years and years. For his brain, for his mind, how he understood things. He wrote very well, very well. But there are a lot of good writers. What I liked is that he seemed to—he had a close language and personal feeling for people that he was—I met him a couple of times. He was a boring old man. But his characters were extraordinary. I mean, I'm sure he wasn't that way to his friends, but you know, I sort of like that. He wasn't all, sort of—I've met writers who were very much [deepens her voice] *writers.* And they were always showing off. [*Laughs*] Nice people but, you know, they're always putting their writing skills above everything else.

ELKANN: Do you think that Black literature is very much alive today?

MORRISON: Well, let me think. I think it's moved—you know, there was a time when the music of Black people was the most important thing. And then it became, sometimes, you know, with some of the writers, with their novels, that Black writing

---

*   Erskine Caldwell (1903–1987) was an American novelist and short story writer, best known for his novel *Tobacco Road.*

became important. Like, um, James Baldwin. So now, it's nothing to single out. It's sort of here . . . But it moved from music, finally, to literature—Black literature, or literature about Black people. Although people like Baldwin, they didn't even live here. He lived in Turkey or someplace.

ELKANN: And you think literature is alive today, you read new books and—

MORRISON: I do! [*Laughs*] I'm not sure if in a large group, or not . . .

ELKANN: Are there any interesting, any new, interesting writers?

MORRISON: Some young women. You know, they're like a new breed of writer because they have some different things they're interested in.

ELKANN: Women have made big progress.

MORRISON: I think so, yeah. Yeah, yeah, yeah. Absolutely.

ELKANN: What do you worry about?

MORRISON: I'm really worried about the man who runs this country.* He's so ignorant, so craven, and shallow, egocentric, vengeful . . . He's an old man. He's 72. He should stop it. I don't know, there's a really great book over here about him that

---

*   At the time of this interview, Donald Trump was president.

Woodward* wrote, called *Fear*. I read that and said *Oh, God*. [*Laughs*] It's worse than I thought! And I thought bad things.

ELKANN: There are reasons to be happy for you?

MORRISON: Yeah. I've lived a long life. It's good.

ELKANN: And you keep on writing?

MORRISON: Oh, yeah.

---

* Bob Woodward, a journalist for the *Washington Post*, who has authored many books profiling presidential administrations, most famously *All the President's Men*, co-authored with Carl Bernstein, about the Nixon administration.

TONI MORRISON was born Chloe Ardelia Wofford (her nickname Toni would come from her baptismal name, Anthony) in Lorain, Ohio. After graduating from Howard University, and getting a master's at Cornell University, she became an English professor, first at Texas Southern University, then back at Howard. When her marriage to Harold Morrison broke up in 1964, leaving her with their two sons, she decided to change careers. Morrison got a job at Random House as the company's first African American fiction editor. She would go on to work with many notable authors, including Angela Davis, Muhammad Ali, and Toni Cade Bambara. Simultaneously, she began working on her own writing, and in 1970 would publish her first novel, *The Bluest Eye*. The book was extremely well received, as was her second novel, *Sula*, and her third novel, *Song of Solomon*, won the National Book Critics Circle Award. She would go on to write several more novels—perhaps most notably, *Beloved*—as well as plays and poetry, and in 1993 she was awarded the Nobel Prize in Literature.

LILA FREILICHER is a long-time publishing industry executive whom, at the time of this interview, was an associate editor at *Publishers Weekly*.

DONALD M. SUGGS JR. (1961–2012) was a senior editor at *The Village Voice*, associate director at the Gay & Lesbian Alliance Against Defamation, and a program director at Harlem United Community AIDS Center.

CHARLAYNE HUNTER-GAULT has been a beat reporter for *The New York Times*, a columnist for *The New Yorker*, a correspondent for PBS, and a bureau chief for NPR. Her work has won numerous awards, including a Peabody Award two Emmys, and the 1986 Journalist of the Year Award from the National Association of Black Journalists.

BILL MOYERS became a journalist after being press secretary to President Lyndon Johnson, starting as publisher of *Newsday*, then, in 1971, beginning a long association with PBS, hosting news and cultural affairs programs. He also spent ten years as a commentator for CBS News. Moyers has won over 30 Emmy awards, three George Polk Awards, a lifetime Peabody Award, and the Walter Cronkite Award for Excellence in Journalism.

ZIA JAFFREY is the author of *The Invisibles: A Tale of the Eunuchs of India*, published in 1996. She lives in New York City.

CAMILLE O. COSBY is a theatrical and television producer, perhaps best known for co-producing the play and subsequent film of the hit *Having Our Say: The Delany Sisters' First 100 Years*. She is also the longtime manager of her husband, comedian Bill Cosby.

CHRISTOPHER BOLLEN is the former editor-in-chief of *Interview Magazine*, and has been an arts journalist for numerous publications, including *Artforum* and *The New York Times*. He is the author of four novels: *Lightning People*, *Orient*, *The Destroyers*, and *A Beautiful Crime*.

ALAIN ELKANN is an Italian journalist who writes a weekly column for the Turin newspaper, *La Stampa*. The host of several cultural programs on Italian TV, he is also the author of several novels, including *Anita* and *Money Must Stay in the Family.*

THE LAST INTERVIEW SERIES

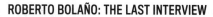

KURT VONNEGUT: THE LAST INTERVIEW

"I think it can be tremendously refreshing if a creator of literature has something on his mind other than the history of literature so far. Literature should not disappear up its own asshole, so to speak."

$15.95 / $17.95 CAN
978-1-61219-090-7
ebook: 978-1-61219-091-4

JACQUES DERRIDA: THE LAST INTERVIEW
LEARNING TO LIVE FINALLY

"I am at war with myself, it's true, you couldn't possibly know to what extent... I say contradictory things that are, we might say, in real tension; they are what construct me, make me live, and will make me die."

translated by PASCAL-ANNE BRAULT and MICHAEL NAAS

$15.95 / $17.95 CAN
978-1-61219-094-5
ebook: 978-1-61219-032-7

ROBERTO BOLAÑO: THE LAST INTERVIEW

"Posthumous: It sounds like the name of a Roman gladiator, an unconquered gladiator. At least that's what poor Posthumous would like to believe. It gives him courage."

translated by SYBIL PEREZ and others

$15.95 / $17.95 CAN
978-1-61219-095-2
ebook: 978-1-61219-033-4

THE LAST INTERVIEW SERIES

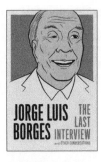

JORGE LUIS BORGES: THE LAST INTERVIEW

"Believe me: the benefits of blindness have been greatly exaggerated. If I could see, I would never leave the house, I'd stay indoors reading the many books that surround me."

translated by KIT MAUDE

$15.95 / $15.95 CAN
978-1-61219-204-8
ebook: 978-1-61219-205-5

HANNAH ARENDT: THE LAST INTERVIEW

"There are no dangerous thoughts for the simple reason that thinking itself is such a dangerous enterprise."

$15.95 / $15.95 CAN
978-1-61219-311-3
ebook: 978-1-61219-312-0

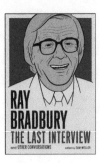

RAY BRADBURY: THE LAST INTERVIEW

"You don't have to destroy books to destroy a culture. Just get people to stop reading them."

$15.95 / $15.95 CAN
978-1-61219-421-9
ebook: 978-1-61219-422-6

THE LAST INTERVIEW SERIES

JAMES BALDWIN: THE LAST INTERVIEW

"You don't realize that you're intelligent until it gets you into trouble."

$15.95 / $15.95 CAN
978-1-61219-400-4
ebook: 978-1-61219-401-1

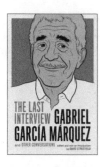

GABRIEL GÁRCIA MÁRQUEZ: THE LAST INTERVIEW

"The only thing the Nobel Prize is good for is not having to wait in line."

$15.95 / $15.95 CAN
978-1-61219-480-6
ebook: 978-1-61219-481-3

LOU REED: THE LAST INTERVIEW

"Hubert Selby. William Burroughs. Allen Ginsberg. Delmore Schwartz... I thought if you could do what those writers did and put it to drums and guitar, you'd have the greatest thing on earth."

$15.95 / $15.95 CAN
978-1-61219-478-3
ebook: 978-1-61219-479-0

THE LAST INTERVIEW SERIES

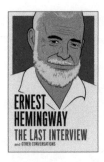

ERNEST HEMINGWAY: THE LAST INTERVIEW

"The most essential gift for a good writer is a built-in, shockproof shit detector."

$15.95 / $20.95 CAN
978-1-61219-522-3
ebook: 978-1-61219-523-0

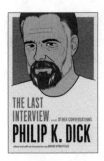

PHILIP K. DICK: THE LAST INTERVIEW

"The basic thing is, how frightened are you of chaos? And how happy are you with order?"

$15.95 / $20.95 CAN
978-1-61219-526-1
ebook: 978-1-61219-527-8

NORA EPHRON: THE LAST INTERVIEW

"You better *make* them care about what you think. It had better be quirky or perverse or thoughtful enough so that you hit some chord in them. Otherwise, it doesn't work."

$15.95 / $20.95 CAN
978-1-61219-524-7
ebook: 978-1-61219-525-4

THE LAST INTERVIEW SERIES

JANE JACOBS: THE LAST INTERVIEW

"I would like it to be understood that all our human economic achievements have been done by ordinary people, not by exceptionally educated people, or by elites, or by supernatural forces."

$15.95 / $20.95 CAN
978-1-61219-534-6
ebook: 978-1-61219-535-3

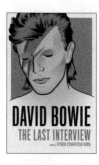

DAVID BOWIE: THE LAST INTERVIEW

"I have no time for glamour. It seems a ridiculous thing to strive for ... A clean pair of shoes should serve quite well."

$16.99 / $22.99 CAN
978-1-61219-575-9
ebook: 978-1-61219-576-6

MARTIN LUTHER KING, JR.: THE LAST INTERVIEW

"Injustice anywhere is a threat to justice everywhere."

$15.99 / $21.99 CAN
978-1-61219-616-9
ebook: 978-1-61219-617-6

THE LAST INTERVIEW SERIES

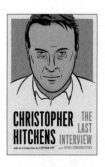

CHRISTOPHER HITCHENS: THE LAST INTERVIEW

"If someone says I'm doing this out of faith, I say,
Why don't you do it out of conviction?"

$15.99 / $20.99 CAN
978-1-61219-672-5
ebook: 978-1-61219-673-2

HUNTER S. THOMPSON: THE LAST INTERVIEW

"I feel in the mood to write a long weird story—a tale
so strange and terrible that it will change the brain
of the normal reader forever."

$15.99 / $20.99 CAN
978-1-61219-693-0
ebook: 978-1-61219-694-7

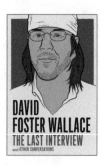

DAVID FOSTER WALLACE: THE LAST INTERVIEW
AND OTHER CONVERSATIONS

"I'm a typical American. Half of me is dying to give
myself away, and the other half is continually
rebelling."

$16.99 / 21.99 CAN
978-1-61219-741-8
ebook: 978-1-61219-742-5

THE LAST INTERVIEW SERIES

KATHY ACKER: THE LAST INTERVIEW AND OTHER CONVERSATIONS

"To my mind I was in a little cage in the zoo
that instead of 'monkey' said 'female
American radical.'"

$15.99 / $20.99 CAN
978-1-61219-731-9
ebook: 978-1-61219-732-6

PRINCE: THE LAST INTERVIEW AND OTHER CONVERSATIONS

"That's what you want. Transcendence.
When that happens—oh, boy."

$16.99 / $22.99 CAN
978-1-61219-745-6
ebook: 978-1-61219-746-3

JULIA CHILD: THE LAST INTERVIEW AND OTHER CONVERSATIONS

"I'm not a chef, I'm a teacher and a cook."

$16.99 / $22.99 CAN
978-1-61219-733-3
ebook: 978-1-61219-734-0

THE LAST INTERVIEW SERIES

URSULA K. LE GUIN: THE LAST INTERVIEW AND OTHER CONVERSATIONS

"Resistance and change often begin in art.
Very often in our art, the art of words."

$16.99 / $21.99 CAN
978-1-61219-779-1
ebook: 978-1-61219-780-7